JAPANESE MARTIAL ARTS

SENSEI NEIL HORTON

summersdale

JAPANESE MARTIAL ARTS

Summersdale Publishers Ltd

46 West Street

Chichester

West Sussex

PO19 1RP

UK

www.summersdale.com

Printed and bound in Great Britain

ISBN 1 84024 478 X

Illustrations by Dan West

CONTENTS

FOREWORD

I began the study of the martial arts in the mid 1970s. The first club I enrolled into was based in Smethwick in the West Midlands under the tutelage and guidance of Sensei Smith and the Budo of Great Britain. I have many fond memories of this club and it is from there that my love for the martial arts began. I was fortunate to gain a deep understanding of various Japanese martial art forms. I have always enjoyed researching what I am doing and there is a wealth of information available on Japanese martial arts.

It would be inappropriate for me not to mention those that had to labour hard for me to be in a position to attend the numerous classes, pay for examinations, travelling fees and other associated costs that accrue. My parents, Joan and Colin, worked very hard to support three children. Their sole aim in life was to provide for their offspring and to give them all the support and guidance a young family needed. It would have been easy for my father to work five days a week and give me an average life, but he would often work seven days a week with my mother in support to allow us the opportunity to have whatever was required financially. My brother, Dean, was a gifted musician and he had private guitar lessons where my father would also attend to learn the theory side of this skill to offer further support. My sister, Debbie, had a sporting talent for netball and hockey and again my father would watch as often as possible. My parents gave their children not only the financial support, but more importantly, the encouragement to strive to do one's best. Without them this book would not have been.

Today my time is split between the martial arts and family life. My wife, Sharon, has had to put up with a lot of my time being spent elsewhere, usually teaching or writing. My children, Ross, Rees and Nathan, have also not had it easy as they have had to share my time also.

Over the last three decades or so, the martial arts in this country have changed. The teaching and training fashions have altered as students have themselves become teachers. Generally, lessons used to be hard work, both mentally and physically, whereas today, this is not so much the case. One thing is for sure, the martial arts will inevitably evolve further. Whether this is for better or worse, only time will tell.

INTRODUCTION

Every nation throughout the world has its own particular history of war or clan rivalry. Historians have for centuries documented the results of war and the reasons behind them. As a consequence of war, leaders and generals have elected to strengthen their armies through processes of education, some crude and some more elaborate. Fighting expertise has gone hand in hand with the tactical calculations of war. In other words, advantage of numbers is not always a recipe for success on the battlefield. Skills and tactical knowledge can outweigh the size of the foe depending upon the expertise gained.

Speaking from my own experience, I have always held the Asian fighting forms and methods in the utmost regard, in particular, the ways of the Japanese. I have been a martial artist and scholar of these forms for over thirty years, and have been exposed to ju-jitsu, karate, atemi-jutsu and judo. Having participated in and taught these arts to a high level, I consequently have great respect for them, their history and origins. Asian fighting methods can be traced back to over seven thousand years ago with the 'kshatriya' or the warrior classes of India. These ancient fighting methods have developed and been in a constant evolutionary state since then. Each confrontation may lead to different perspectives and encourage further learning.

When I decided to write this book, there were many obstacles in the way and years of research were required as text and information is not always readily available covering all of the martial art forms. I wanted to introduce the Japanese martial arts to a wider audience, and felt that an easy-to-read guide to various forms was the best way to achieve this. There are many in-depth studies on individual forms available, and I hope that this book will provide an overview of these fascinating combat techniques, and that readers will want to seek out more information on the ones that interest them the most.

Fighting forms often pre-date the introduction of firearms and allied explosive devices. Even today many Japanese methods of combat are more akin to those of ancient times and the feudal era, and it is the early forms that provide a deeper understanding of why and how a particular method would be used. Such forms have spawned their own splinter forms and ultimately the second generation would lead to third and fourth generations of variations. Over the centuries many branches have evolved, and indeed, still continue to do so.

When we consider all the Japanese islands, there is a multitude of fighting forms that have existed and still exist today. Some have become obsolete whilst others have modified themselves into several branches of the same form. Some contain weaponry, some contain no weaponry and others use a mixture of the two. To discuss them all would require many books. I have, therefore, chosen to select some of the well known and some of the less common, in an attempt to demonstrate the variety that exists. I must point out there are many more martial arts that have originated in Japan than can be covered in this book. Moreover, I have tried to summarise the ones I have covered in order to give the reader an accessible overview, rather than go into too much detail here about any one form.

INTRODUCTION

Military arts were devised for one purpose, and one purpose alone: the protection of the individual and his kin. There was an overwhelming desire to acquire the knowledge and skills needed to accomplish this. In times of brutality and merciless aggression, such fighting skills were paramount. There were certain periods during Japanese history, when the students, often farmers or peasants, would have to go into isolation to learn the fighting forms due to the fact that they had been banned by stronger armies or opposing forces, who saw the development of these skills as a threat to their dominance. Small villages and towns were often the target for exploitation and subjection by such forces, making fighting skills a must.

Japanese history is peppered with many wars and clan disputes. Internal warfare was rife. Battles were not restricted to the ruling classes, but there was often rivalry amongst towns and villages too. Peasants and farmers alike were involved in some way in the outcome of the struggles. Often, the peasants had no alternative other than to use their tools of trade as their weapon.

One important period in Japanese history is the rise of the samurai. The samurai serve as an excellent example of how feudal troubles were constantly evident in Japan, from the Heian period (794–1185) right up to 1868, when the feudal era ended. The samurai were members of the warrior class, which was at the top of the social hierarchy, and they were originally fighters who were hired by landowners to protect their property and ensure that the farmers and peasants were controlled. The samurai received fighting tuition in schools, known as '*ryu*'. Here, there were many combat skills to be learnt and military leaders would fervently support these *ryu*. The incredible rise in the number of schools scattered over the Japanese islands was a direct result of the need to learn these skills. Demand was so great that by seventeenth century AD, over nine thousand *ryu* were recorded in existence. Samurai followed a strict, ethical code that was heavily influenced by Confucian beliefs; elements that were important included loyalty to one's master, self-discipline and honour. The samurai were famed for their swordsmanship but they also used other weapons such as spears. Jujutsu is the martial art that the samurai invented, and as we will see later, this remains one of the most popular Japanese martial arts.

So how do the modern martial arts have links with the past? Firstly, Asian values and beliefs have been passed on through the generations of martial arts. Instructors will pass on such beliefs and ideologies as they form part of the core of their form. The Japanese are firm believers of respect, discipline, etiquette and military chivalry, to name just a few elements. Such virtues are enforced by some instructors which can often have a negative result on the class size. Many Japanese rituals and ways can be difficult to accept for the westerner, but this can be overcome with time.

Religion and spiritual doctrine are also key features with many Japanese martial arts as they too have trickled through the learning process, as they have in Korean and Chinese forms. Principally, Buddhism, Zen and Shintoism are the major driving forces. Examining these doctrines can assist with the understanding of the creation and core values of a particular martial art. I have provided a very brief summary of Buddhism, Zen and Shintoism below, as these are the most important spiritual influences on the Japanese martial arts.

Buddhism is one of the largest and most followed of all religions today. Millions of followers adhere to its principles and uphold its teachings. Buddhists believe they will attain enlightenment by following a set path of teachings. To avoid heading in the wrong direction or straying from the path, a series of instructions have been laid down.

Buddhists do not have a god. An individual's life after death is said to be dictated through a direct result of one's karma. It is believed the individual will ascend through the planes of existence if they remain true to the teachings. The karma acts in a similar way to a ladder of judgement and the higher one climbs the ladder is determined by the way they conduct their life.

So what are the Buddhist guidelines? The first set of principles are known as the Eightfold Path and this guides followers to achieve the aims of Buddhism through the right understanding, the right resolve, the right speech and action, the right effort and livelihood, together with the right mindfulness and meditation.

Zen is a branch of Buddhism that originated in China but has since spread through Japan and Asia to the rest of the world. The creation of Zen is attributed to an Indian sage and teacher, Bodhodharma. He is believed to have links with the martial arts through the famous Shaolin temples, where he was a practising monk. According to martial arts history, Bodhodharma developed a series of exercises to improve the physical and mental well-being of the monks, which then developed into fighting forms. Traditionally, monasteries and temples have always been important in the history of martial arts because many warriors sought refuge in them. They were able to practise and improve their techniques and were influenced by the teachings and beliefs of the monks. With the ideology of Zen, one can attain enlightenment without the use of scriptures or formalised text. Meditation is significant and there is a belief that people can become self-reliant and increase their overall strength of character. Nature is very important to this doctrine, and followers are taught to respect and live in harmony with it. The practice of Zen is said to alleviate fear, which can only be beneficial to the martial artist.

Shintoism was once the state religion of Japan, and as such, the foundations of it are based on a belief in the superiority of Japan and the Japanese emperor. Although it was abolished as the state religion after the Second World War, its traditions and customs are still very important in Japanese society, although the nationalistic aspects have diminished in popularity.

Like Zen, one of the most important features of this religion is the high level of respect and devotion that is shown towards nature. In modern times, many aspects of Shintoism are seen as folk customs rather than an actual religion, and many Japanese Buddhists incorporate Shinto practises into their lives. In fact, Shintoism and Buddhism have always co-existed in Japan and it can be difficult to make clear distinctions between the two.

Shintoism teaches people to love and respect nature, to only kill other living beings when absolutely necessary and to always be grateful for a creature giving its life to feed and clothe them. Many cultural customs that are typically Japanese are based on Shinto practises and in the martial arts world, one of the clearest links to this belief system is in the sport of Sumo Wrestling. Many rituals associated with Sumo Wrestling are formed on the basis on Shinto teachings, such as sprinkling the arena with salt before a match, which is believed to purify the area.

Today, martial arts schools have strict codes of conduct that must be followed by the student. Pupils are effectively tutored in the exactness of technique or the application of salutation. Specific martial arts carry obligatory bowing rituals and ceremonies to one's teacher, known as 'sensei', and to the opponent, and even the place that practice takes place. The rules may slightly deviate from one school to the next, but respect and etiquette are always given the utmost importance.

One question that should always be addressed when researching a martial art is why was such a form created? The Japanese martial arts have always inspired historians because the islands have been involved in many battles and clan wars, both internally and from foreign foes. The Japanese even created a warrior code known as '*bushido*', detailing how warriors should conduct themselves in war and in everyday life. The mentality and psychology of a warrior can be linked with the way in which he conducts his life or how he perceives life itself. The Japanese concept of death for their country can be clearly seen with the kamikaze pilots of the Second World War, where the pilot's sole goal was to give his life for the nation and emperor.

The difficulty in compiling a book of this nature is the sheer wealth of styles to choose from and then deciding on which ones to cover. One should also understand that many martial forms were taught in isolation from the outside world and restricted to the eyes of the extended family. This comes to the fore when an author attempts to trace the genealogy of a particular martial art. Often hearsay and flamboyant claims can block the truth and lead one in the wrong direction.

I have compiled a number of Japanese martial arts and listed them in alphabetical order. Each form is summarised and aimed at giving a general idea of what the style is about.

A BRIEF NOTE
ON KATA

Japanese martial arts have specific themes that are taught from the offset. One major characteristic is the instruction of 'kata'. Kata is a Japanese term that refers to a pattern of movements that one performs in order to practice a particular style. Kata are predetermined moves that enable the student to learn the correct way to stand, block, punch kick and even breath. They aid in the uniformity of a style and also assist in the preservation of a martial doctrine.

The subject of kata has been very controversial, however, revealing disagreement between members of the martial arts fraternity. There are those of the traditionalist view that avidly promote the significance of kata, or, 'prearranged sequence', and those that favour a sporting or competition fighting format.

Many schools of martial art have some kind of kata to use as a learning tool or process for the pupil. Karate disciplines have a vast quantity and will commence the study of the early days. The majority are given names and the sequence has largely remained intact from the original theme. Korean martial arts have developed their own unique kata, which are called either *'hyung'* or *'poomse'*.

Kata has a worldwide training package and standards can be judged and evaluated at international competitions. Certain disciplines will apply kata in grading and other ranking examinations too. The kata are performed either solo or in pairs, depending upon the individual requirements of a combat establishment. When one investigates the karate kata the influence of Okinawa will be increasingly evident with progression. The principal schools that assisted in the creation of the kata are the Naha-te, the Shuri-te and the Tomari-te.

AIKIDO

The term *'aiki'* literally means 'harmony meeting' or 'spirit meeting' and the word *'do'* is employed to suggest a 'way' or 'path'. Therefore, Aikido translates as 'way of harmony or spirit meeting' The late Morihei Ueshiba founded this martial art in the 1930s.

Ueshiba gained an early education in the martial arts from the famous Daito-ryu headed by Sokaku Takeda. It is believed Daito-ryu gave Ueshiba his technical expertise and practical mastery. He dedicated his time and efforts into fine-tuning what was to become Aikido. Ueshiba became devoted to his studies and trained constantly in amassing and trying to perfect his knowledge, both physically and spiritually.

Morihei Ueshiba was an acclaimed exponent of the sword and allied traditional weaponry of that era. The philosophy of Aikido owes much to the Shinto and Zen faiths that were prominent in his way of life. Nature is extremely significant in Ueshiba's Aikido along with natural movements. Ueshiba favoured natural movement and believed one could achieve a better state of self defence by using it. In conjunction with Shintoism, it puts an emphasis on tradition and the past, especially traditions with feudal connections. However, Ueshiba also became a devout follower of the 'new religion' of Omotokyo that was in part neo-Shintoism and in part socio-political idealism. He was a very spiritually orientated master.

Aikido is predominantly a non-resistant form, and the concept of non-aggressive movement and technique is rooted within the way and paramount to its being. Aikido is largely based around using the opponent's strength, stature and balance against him. Such an importance given to the ideal of non-aggression makes it almost a pure method of self-defence. Morihei Ueshiba taught the notion and the practise of circular movement to evade and eventually defeat the opponent. The concept is to be victorious by utilising little force and by evasive actions.

Like other martial art forms, Aikido relies upon the principle of using the opponent's strength and speed to the advantage of the defender. The defender needs to be flexible in thought and practise and be in total control of their technique. There is a requirement for perfect timing and knowledge of how to overcome the foe. Ueshiba believed and proved that understanding the opponent is vital and will inevitably be conclusive in a real life scenario.

To enhance the prospect of victory, the student of this particular martial art is educated in the means of internal vital energy or 'ki'; knowing how to strengthen both the spirit and the physical being in an attempt to synchronise the two. Harmony is an integral part of the study of Aikido.

Morihei Ueshiba rapidly gained disciples in his homeland after eventually giving his style a name in 1938. Word of the skill and technical competence of Ueshiba was spreading throughout the Japanese islands. He incorporated strong elements of spiritual study as well as the obvious defensive techniques. Ueshiba was devoutly philosophical and spiritually orientated throughout his life. He spent much of his life attempting to ascertain moral and correct judgement that one could both readily apply. He would openly pass on his mental doctrine and demonstrate his spiritual prowess.

Today, Aikido is spreading throughout the globe, but probably not as rapidly as the less ritual-based styles. Aikido demands more of a mental attitude and respect for traditional values and etiquette than many other popular martial arts. Etiquette is extremely important and strongly adhered to. The correct salutation, or bowing rituals, are sternly enforced and performed by all, regardless of their status in the school.

An individual's rank is indicated by the means of a coloured belt system. The black belt levels or tiers are classed as the master levels. Traditional practice uniform, or 'gi', is worn and the Aikido student at a predetermined grade has the right to wear a *'hakama'*, or traditional divided skirt. Again, the wearing of the *hakama* is a sympathetic alliance with the Japanese warrior class, known as samurai.

Aikido is a martial art that uses joint-locks and throws to subdue an attacker. The focus of the locks is based around the wrist, or *'kote'*, and the elbow, known as *'empi'*. The defender, known as *'tori'*, is taught how to twist and apply the right pressure to the joint areas. The vulnerable regions and the nerve strikes are combined with the knowledge of where and how to strike the opponent to acquire the best outcome. In fact, despite the system's emphasis on fine motor-skill grappling methods Ueshiba claimed, 'ninety-nine per cent of Aikido is atemi'. ('Atemi' comes from two Japanese terms, '*ate*' meaning strike or striking, and '*mi*' meaning the body; therefore atemi means body-strikes or -striking.) Much practice and theory is used to learn how to render an attacker or attackers immobile.

Defensive stance and how one should evade a particular attack are covered in great detail. The idea is to rapidly repel an attacker, either unarmed or carrying a weapon. The layman may first perceive a system that looks graceful and holds little strength. The actual pain that can be inflicted from an aikido lock is, however, to be respected.

Aikido is mainly an unarmed study but a general syllabus could also cover the stick, known as a '*jo*', and knife, or '*tanto*', as well as the sword. The objective is to widen the defensive role-plays of the students and to create a comprehensive system.

Another area where aikido has gathered admirers is its effective manner of defending against multiple attackers. The training package is geared towards understanding body mechanics and how a delivery of an assault can be predicted by the way in which the anatomy moves . The training ideal is to develop an instinct that can forecast how and where a specific blow will land.

There are more than a score of aikido groups or branches that exist today. The more notable establishments include: Minoru Hirai's Korindo Aikido, Kenji Tomiki's system and Gozo Shioda's style known as Yoshinkan. Each aforementioned master developed a divergence from the true core; however, Morihei Ueshiba's ways and beliefs are still the prevailing method.

AIKI-JUTSU

Aiki-jutsu is considered to be one of Japan's oldest established martial arts, having a lineage that stretches back over nearly a thousand years. The origins of aiki-jutsu can be traced back to the Japanese Kamakura Shogunate era which dates from 1185–1333 AD (sometimes listed as 1192–1333 AD as there is dispute amongst historians as to the exact dates). Japanese warriors, or *'bushi'*, of that era and beyond adopted aiki-jutsu.

Roughly defined, aiki-jutsu is an unarmed warrior art closely linked to the aiki ju-jutsu taught by the famous military arts establishment Daito-ryu. Like its modern-day successor, aiki-jutsu is usually represented as a grappling-based art using an opponent's aggression against them and has a bias towards the manipulation of the wrist joint. At the core of the system lies the philosophy of blending both attack and defence. Aiki-jutsu, or, 'art of harmonious spirit', was crucial to the survival of the warrior and his kin alike. The aiki-jutsu student would learn the necessary knowledge of the weaker areas of the attackers anatomy and how best to immobilise or restrain the potential confrontation. They were educated on how and where to strike at the opponent with the hands and feet to gain maximum advantage, a section of their training known as *'atemi-waza'*, and combine this with joint-lock techniques, known as *'kansetsu-waza'*, and throwing procedures, known as *'nage-waza'*. The ideology was to provide a comprehensive means of both attack and defence.

Each pupil would be required to have an understanding of how to apply defensive situations to weapon wielding foes. There is a necessity for the student to acquire speed and precision when first dodging and then counterattacking. Like most martial arts, the goal is to create a state of natural reflex action, which would serve best the purposes of the student and master alike.

Much of the aiki-jutsu theorems have been absorbed into other Japanese fighting methods. The success and popularity of the art served to give this discipline a status amongst other fields of an allied nature. Aiki-jutsu joint-locking techniques were readily adopted by other forms for their effectiveness; the samurai were exponents of this style and other forms have followed suit. The art is still practised today, but often in an environment that promotes more *do* than *jutsu* aspects. It is true to say that the popularity has dwindled with the rise of more modern or sport orientated schools of thought. Western views and customs have brought about martial arts that offer prizes and monetary rewards, and many potential students have followed the capitalist ideology, staying away from traditional ways. The traditional Japanese values of chivalry, respect and honour are still at the very core of this art.

ATEMI-JUTSU

The specialised art of atemi-jutsu comes from the Japanese translation for 'art of body-strikes'. The system encompasses a vast array of methods than can be utilised to attack many different areas of the aggressor's body. The overall objective of the student of Atemi-jutsu is to gain either immobilisation or the complete destruction of one's counterpart.

Through knowledge of the nerve areas and body mechanics, selected areas of the opponent's body can be exposed and deliberately targeted to produce a variety of responses. The student needs to know how the nervous system works and what results can be obtained by striking a specific region with a specific body part. The student is closely supervised when in the 'dojo' or training hall. Lethal movements can be demonstrated and imitated though not actually performed in the classroom environment on the understanding that they are not utilised in play. Instructors tend, however, to keep these secrets to the more advanced student or shy away from displaying them to any great extent.

One will find that other modern martial forms have borrowed the theories and the knowledge of atemi, or 'body-strikes'. Atemi-jutsu can necessitate a long study programme before one can be fully conversant with it. Modern medicine has assisted in the further understanding how the nervous system, known in Japanese as *'shinkei keito'*, works in the context of combat. Surprising to some is how much the ancient masters did know. This is well documented and their findings have been passed onto future generations of students.

Atemi-jutsu students will acquire a specialised knowledge of the body-strikes, for instance, the eye, ear, temple, nose, mouth, chin, cheekbone, throat, solar plexus, chest, stomach, groin region, thigh, knee, shin, toes and ankle. They will advance to a greater understanding of how to expose certain regions and how to twist the joint and crush the nerve centres, for example.

Atemi-jutsu is mainly taught as a companion area of study to Daito-ryu and aiki-jutsu derived schools such as aikido and Hakko-ryu Ju-jutsu. Therefore to speculate on the global membership of atemi-justu students would be impossible. Despite many claims it is rarely, if at all, taught as a pure discipline. Many aspects and features of atemi-jutsu have been radically added to and developed into other martial arts. It is clear that the knowledge of how and where to strike is important in the vast majority of martial arts, both past and present, and not restricted to those of a Japanese extraction.

BU-JUTSU

Bu-jutsu is a general term and stems from the Japanese translation of 'military arts'. The Japanese have created numerous distinctive and individual fighting forms. Students either mix their forms or stay aligned to one teaching. As we have seen, the initiation and conception of the combat methods grew from the need of self-preservation and that of their kin and their surrounding community.

The warrior, or '*bushi*', was seen as being more useful to the clan or family, known as '*daimyo*', if they were skillful in the art of combat. Military fighting forms were subject to a rapid growth and explosion in feudal times, when family and clan disputes were common and the fighting ability of the warriors could determine the outcome of war. Bu-jutsu signifies the martial arts of both unarmed and weapon skills and/or a mixture of the two components. In eras where hand-to-hand combat was common, be it domestic disputes, duelling or on the battlefield, the science of warfare was based on daily occurrences and much research and development was spent on obtaining functional, effective fighting skills.

The spiritual and mental understanding was additionally geared towards that of war. For example, military chivalry is an ingredient in Japan's indigenous religion of Shintoism. Japanese thinking was centred on the way of war and the way the physical and the mental strengths can interact, similar to the concept of the kamikazi in the Second World War.

To understand the doctrine is to comprehend the significance of the combat skills that follow. The two components run hand in hand with each other. When the mental and physical pursuits and attributes were connected a code was created known as *bushido*, or 'warrior way or path'. *Bushido* was a code of military chivalry and a code of everyday conduct rolled into one. Ethics and devotion were a manner of demonstrating one's allegiance to the *daimyo* chieftains and the community as a whole.

Bu-jutsu was a part of everyday life, a routine that was paramount. Even in times of peace, military training was still in demand in case disputes should arise at a later date, which they usually did. These military ways would play a major role in the life of the Japanese warrior and they rapidly evolved as more and more knowledge was gathered and understood. Bu-jutsu essentially became budo during the Meiji era (1867–1912) when Japan recreated itself in peacetime by opening up to the west and making huge technological advances. The samurai were no longer permitted to carry their swords in public and the martial arts became more to do with personal development than systems for use in battle. Thus ken-jutsu became kendo, iai-jutsu became iaido, kyu-jutsu became kyudo and so on.

IAIDO

Iaido is a traditional Japanese martial art form that translates into 'way of the sword'. The method was a development from the more ancient method of 'iai-jutsu' or 'art of the sword'. The Japanese have always been admirers of and have even worshipped their weaponry, none more so than the sword. Therefore most samurai or warrior classes were apt swordsmen and many samurai won a legendary status. The warrior classes of Japan's feudal period were instrumental in the creation of many different martial arts that are still practised today, and iaido, largely unchanged over the years from its traditional source, is one of the traditional weapon arts.

Iaido provides a disciplined system for the methodical way in which the exponent draws the Japanese sword. There is a set standard to how this should be performed. Additionally, the martial artist observes how the weapon is drawn from its scabbard. The accuracy and precision of movement are monitored and corrected where necessary by instructors, known as sensei.

Iaido is largely performed for aesthetic and spiritual appreciation with very little real combat intent. The unsheathing of the weapon known as 'nukitsuke' must adhere to strict guidelines and also to its return to the scabbard, called 'noto'. Another technique includes the manner of shaking off the blood called 'chiburi' and the actual cut called 'kiritsuke'. The most common design of sword that students of iaido use and base their kata, or set movements, around is the 'katana', a type of sword worn through the 'obi', or belt, with the blade facing up.

The iaidoka (a practitioner of iaido) will typically commence the kata, from a seated position, known as 'seiza' (although some schools, most notably the modern military discipline of Toyama-ryu, do their entire series of katas standing). The iaidoka will then rise and release the sword from the scabbard with the use of the thumb. Whilst the scabbard is turned to enable the sword to be brought to its tip, the student rises so that the upper parts

of the legs are straight. When the sword leaves the scabbard, the exponent will stamp the foot and the scabbard is thrust back and the blade will simultaneously cut forward. The student will then move in a forward direction and thrust the scabbard forward too. The weapon is then raised above the head and the action is to cut downwards. Stages of shaking off the blood follow and the process then moves into the pupil standing on his feet. Finally, the weapon is placed ceremoniously back into the scabbard and the student finishes the exercise.

Iaido clothing is very much in line with that worn in other traditional Japanese martial arts. Students wear a *hakama* split skirt over their '*uwagi*', a variation of the typical loose-fitting martial arts tunic and bottoms, which is very similar in design to the light gi used in arts like karate. Practice is mainly done with a blunt replica of a sword, known as an iaito. As students progress, some invest in the real thing and even go on to practice the art of Tamishi-geri, the art of physically cutting through objects with the sword.

A martial artist's level is judged and measured on the way that they execute the foundations of the form. There are distinct physical and mental codes to be observed. The art of iaido has always attracted a following, which considers the mental aspect to be as important as the physical prowess. Foreign students of this art may find this area cumbersome and at odds with their respective cultures in comparison to students from a typical Japanese iaidoka. Oriental doctrine and beliefs are far removed from their western counterparts. Nevertheless iaido is still quite popular away from its homeland, where it is normally a martial artist's second subject.

JO-JUTSU

A '*jo*' is Japanese terminology for a hardwood stick that measures approximately four feet in length. The actual size, weight and shape may differ according to individual preference. Jo-jutsu is Japanese for 'art of the stick'. The general phrase can be applied to many martial arts that use the stick as a training tool or those that incorporate the practice of stick forms into their syllabus. There are several martial arts that have found the subject of jo-jutsu an aid to their style, for a variety of reasons.

The founder of the most well known self-contained method is said by some to be Muso Gonnosuke Katsuyoshi, who founded Shindo Muso-ryu Jo-jutsu, although some historians argue that the way of the stick was a fighting form long before him. Jo-jutsu has had a long tradition and many authorities have claimed that they were the first to integrate it into their combat training. Therefore jo-jutsu has a large collection of specialist drills that are now widely practised.

The stick can be used in several ways. Firstly, the weapon can be utilised both in attack and in defence from another stick or bladed weaponry. It can either be used to jab like a spear or strike in a downward fashion, but probably the most common technique is when the stick is sent in a swinging motion.

Jo-jutsu, like most traditional Japanese martial arts, is often tutored by the means of several kata. The *jo* is a fairly short weapon, when compared to the six foot *bo* staff, which makes it ideal for short-range targets and is a weapon that can generate an enormous amount of speed and power.

There are many targets of the adversary's anatomy that it can attack, but again the principal points are those that are most vulnerable, which include the soft areas or fleshy parts of the body or exposed areas in a soldier's armour. Specific regions include the side and top of the head, most regions of the face, the collarbone, the sides of the chest, the joints of the body, the stomach, the groin and the neck and throat.

The stick can also be used as a blocking device against a blade and there is a legend where Muso Gonnosuke Katsuyoshi defeated the famous samurai swordsman, Myomoto Musashi. Usually the stick creates the block or parry that permits the opportunity for a secondary strike to occur. There are many ways that the stick can be advantageous and the subject of jo-jutsu attempts to cover all feasible possibilities.

One must also note that the stick forms are not solely restricted to the arts of Japan. Many nations use stick forms of combat. The stick was probably one of the first weapons ever to be used in an argument between two opponents or an army of men.

Jo-jutsu can be taught as a martial art in itself, but it is the norm to find it embedded into other combat forms. The Shindo Muso-ryu system goes under the name of jodo since the introduction of budo martial arts in Japan.

JUDO

Judo is fairly modern in its concept and records are easily obtained. There is a great deal of knowledge to learn in judo and it has standardised training drills. Judo is a sport that is practised by all age groups and by both genders.

Judo means 'gentle or flexible way' and is a Japanese martial art form that was created by Jigaro Kano. Kano was born in 1860 and he had been a noted scholar and master of ju-jutsu. His early years were spent training in Kito-ryu and the Tenjin Shinyo-ryu establishments, where he acquired a thirst for further knowledge. The two said ju-jutsu schools were famous for producing many masters of that era.

In 1882 Jigaro Kano commenced the teaching of his own individual ideas that were largely centred on his own experiences and studies. Kano had long been an admirer of techniques and the applications that were of a practical relevance. Originally, he named the establishment the Kodokan Judo.

Kano died in 1938 and left a standardised and structured way behind that is practised in many nations of the world. Judo's success is a monument to Jigaro Kano's dedication and knowledge. It acquired Olympic status at the Tokyo games in 1964, and the sheer size of its overall membership throughout the world is astonishing, such is the popularity and effectiveness of the sport.

Judo techniques can be divided into three main groups or categories. The first, standing techniques, known as 'tachi-waza', include many of the throwing techniques, known as 'nage-waza'. The first group can again be sub-divided into hand techniques, known as 'te-waza', hip techniques, known as 'koshi-waza', leg or foot techniques, known as 'ashi-waza' and 'sutemi-waza', which translates as sacrifice techniques, which are techniques where you place yourself at risk so you can feign the enemy or opponent.

The second principle consists of vital point striking techniques or *atemi-waza*. This category is learnt purely as a form of self-defence and is not allowed in competition. Because of this many modern judoka instructors neglect and purposefully avoid the practice of *atemi-waza*. However, the non-acceptance of *atemi-waza* on the tournament circuit is only one reason. Another can be disagreement over the strike's practical function. *Atemi-waza* can be a very complicated feature and training in it can appear too abstract from training in modern competitive judo. However, the subject is integral to the overall composition of Kodokan Judo.

'Ne-waza', or ground techniques, consists of a series of ways of fighting the opponent on the floor or mat. Again, this can be sub-divided into 'osaekomi-waza', which means holding techniques, 'kansetsu-waza' or locking techniques and 'shime-waza', which translates into strangling techniques. Having the knowledge to fight on the ground has become very popular in the current practice of martial arts. In reality the majority of street confrontations, if not ended within the first few seconds, finish with one or two parties on the floor. Judo is respected for its vast understanding in this particular area of self-defence.

The correct method of breaking one's fall when being thrown is also significant in preventing injury. There are several different types of fall and they are an important part of the training. The term for break-fall, the correct way to land safely following a throw, is 'ukemi'.

Judo favours the competition scene, and the students enter tournaments. The idea is to gain points and ultimately victory over one's opponent. Scores are given for the correct execution of the throws and hold-downs and for the surrender of the adversary. The referee will award the contest to the person with the most points during a predetermined period of time.

Many martial artists are unaware that there are kata contained in judo. The kata are demonstrated in pairs, as with most traditional Japanese grappling-based disciplines. The major kata are: Nage-no-kata, Katame-no-kata, Go-no-sen-no-kata, Kime-no-kata, Itsutsu-no-kata, Ju-no-kata, Koshiki-no-kata and Kodokan-goshin-jutsu.

Training in the class environment will commence with free practice known as '*randori*'. Judo is practised in a training hall known, or *dojo* and performed on a mat, or '*tatami*'. The dress

worn, known as a *'judogiI'*, is traditionally a hardwearing version of Japanese *'dogi'* uniform with padding on the chest and the arm areas. Like other martial arts the grading structure is divided with the use of adorning coloured belts. Kano is considered to be the founder of this popular qualification system.

Nage-no-kata, or forms of throwing, is a composition of fifteen throwing procedures that are divided into three sets of five. The sequence of Nage-no-kata is as follows:

Series one: *te-waza* **(hand techniques)**

Uki-otoshi ~ floating drop

Seoinage ~ shoulder throw

Kata-guruma ~ shoulder wheel

Series two: *koshi-waza* **(hip techniques)**

Uki-goshi ~ floating hip throw

Harai goshi ~ sweeping hip throw

Tsuri-komi-goshi ~ lifting hip throw

Series three: *ashi-waza* **(leg and foot techniques)**

Okuri-ashi-harai ~ sweeping ankle throw

Sasae-tsuri-komi-ashi ~ propping drawing ankle throw

Uchi-mata ~ inner thigh throw

Series four: *sutemi-waza* **(sacrifice techniques)**

Tomoe-nage ~ stomach throw

Ura-nage ~ rear throw

Sumi-gaeshi ~ corner throw

Series five: *yoko-sutemi-waza* **(side sacrifice techniques)**

Yoko-gake ~ side body drop

Yoko-guruma ~ side wheel throw

Uki-waza ~ floating techniques

Katame-no-kata or 'forms of grappling' was created to explore and practise the effective means of holding or immobilising the opponent. The kata is separated into three distinct sections.

Series one: *osae-waza* **(holding techniques)**

Kesa gatame ~ scarf hold

Kata-gatame ~ shoulder hold

Kami-shiho-gatame ~ upper four-corner hold

Yoko-shiho-gatame ~ side four-corner hold

Kuzure-kami-shiho-gatame ~ broken upper four-corner hold

Series two: *shime-waza* **(strangling techniques)**

Kata juji-jime ~ half-cross strangle hold

Hadaka-jime ~ naked choke lock

Okuri eri-jime ~ sliding collar choke

Kata ha-jime ~ single wing choke

Gyaku juji-jime ~ reverse cross strangle hold

Series three: *kansetsu-waza* **(locking techniques)**

Ude-garami ~ entangled arm lock

Juji-gatame ~ cross arm lock

Ude-gatame ~ arm lock

Hiza gatame ~ knee arm lock

Ashi-garami ~ entangled leg lock

The third named prearranged sequence is called Go-no-sen-no-kata. The name translates into forms of counter-throwing and gives the student the knowledge thereof. Pupils of Judo are taught both how to throw the opponent and to counteract the similar situation.

Go-no-sen-no-kata is performed as follows:

Counterattacks

1. Osoto gari Osoto gari

2. Hiza-guruma Hiza-guruma

3. Ouchi-gari De-ashi-harai

4. De-ashi-harai De-ashi-harai

5. Kosoto gake Tai-otoshi

6. Ko-uchi-gari Sasae-tsuri-komi-ashi

7. Kubi-nage Ushiro-goshi

8. Koshi-guruma Uki-goshi

9. Hane-goshi Sasae-tsuri-komi-ashi

10. Harai-goshi Ushiro-goshi

11. Uchi mata Sukui-nage

12. Kata seoinage Sumi-gaeshi

Kime-no-kata is the 'kata of self-defence'. It is divided by two methods of defensive position: *'idori'* (kneeling) and *'tachiai'* (standing). There are eight seated or kneeling defences and twelve standing. Kime-no-kata is as follows:

Idori

Ryote-dori ∼ both hand seizure

Tsuki-kake ∼ straight punch to stomach

Suri-age ∼ blow against forehead with palm

Yoko-uchi ∼ blow at the temple

Ushiro-dori ∼ shoulder grab from rear

Tsuki-komi ∼ knife thrust at stomach

Kiri-komi ∼ direct downward cut with knife

Yoko-tsuki ∼ side thrust with knife

Tachiai

Ryote-dori ~ both hand seizure

Sode-tori ~ side sleeve seizure

Tsuki-kake ~ straight punch to face

Tsuki-age ~ uppercut blow

Suri-age ~ blow against forehead with palm

Yoko-uchi ~ blow at the temple

Keage ~ kick to abdomen

Ushiro-dori ~ shoulder grab from rear

Tsuki-komi ~ stomach thrust with knife

Kiri-komi ~ direct downward cut with knife

Nuki-kake ~ sword unsheathing

Kiri-otoshi ~ direct downward cut with sword

Itsutsu-no-kata translates into 'forms of five'. The sequence uses five principles that were not named by the founder of judo, Jigaro Kano. Ju-no-kata is once again made up of fifteen techniques that are classed into three groups.

Ju-no-kata is as follows:

Series one

Tsuki-dashi ~ hand thrusting

Kata-oshi ~ shoulder push

Ryote-dore ~ two hand seizure

Kata mawashi ~ shoulder turning

Ago-oshi ~ jaw twisting

Series two

Kiri-oroshi ~ direct hand cut with weapon

Ryo-kata-oshi ~ pressing on both shoulders

Nanami-uchi ~ diagonal strike

Katate-dori ~ single hand hold

Katate-age ~ raising hand to strike

Series three

Obi-tori ~ belt seizure

Mune oshi ~ chest punch

Tsuki-age ~ uppercut

Uchi-oroshi ~ direct head strike

Ryogan-tsuki ~ both eyes poke

Koshiki-no-kata or 'forms of antique', is performed with the assumption that one is adorned in armour. The kata is categorised into two modes, *'omote'* or frontal movement and *'ura'* or rear movement.

JU-JUTSU

It is believed by many that the martial art known as ju-jutsu came into being in the thirteenth century AD. Other spellings of ju-jutsu have also been used, for instance, ju-jitsu, ju jitsu, jujutsu, jiu-jutsu and jiu jitsu yet they are referring to the same collection of (usually) grappling-based martial arts. Ju-jutsu is comparable to Chinese kung fu or wu shu, in that it encompasses many different indigenous systems. Having said this, there is a distinct difference between traditional Japanese ju-jutsu and the popular art of Brazilian jiu jitsu (always spelt this way), which is mainly derived from judo.

The most famous schools of ju-jutsu, thanks to the masters and personalities they produced, have been the Takenouchi-ryu, the Tenjin Shinyo-ryu, Sosuishitsu-ryu, Sekiguchi-ryu, Daito-ryu and the Kito-ryu. It seems apparent that each school contained strengths that were beneficial to the overall theme of ju-jutsu. By definition the systems are all primarily focused on grappling unarmed fighting and are derived from the methods of the samurai.

More than seven hundred schools of ju-jutsu have subsequently originated from Japan. If one imagines that from this number other establishments have been propagated – as many pupils have then taken and created their own concepts and changed the name of the original title – then the magnitude of the different methods of ju-jutsu would be huge and immeasurable.

Ju-jutsu, which translates to mean 'the art of flexibility' or 'the art of gentleness', is considered to be the forerunner of many other acclaimed Japanese martial arts such as aikido and judo. Ju-jutsu techniques are as wide ranging as their styles and there are no standardised texts. The many applications include those of kicking hand techniques or *te-waza*, finger techniques or *yubi-waza*, joint-locking or *kansetsu-waza*, strangulation and choking called *shime-waza*, throwing applications that are called *nage-waza*, blocking techniques or *uke-waza* and ground-fighting known as *ne-waza*.

Certain schools have made the addition of teaching weaponry to enhance the traditional and classical link, as well as guidelines for improving the body mechanics of unarmed technique. The weapons include the sword, the staff, the stick and farming tools that were converted into defensive arms. Some teachers have even adopted the art of tying the opponent, known as '*hojo-jutsu*'. *Hoju-jutsu* has strong links to traditional fighting methods and some

ancient forms of ju-jutsu that exist today still hold the practice of this system in high regard.

Ju-jutsu originally catered for the many requirements that were demanded by the samurai. Unarmed combat was a prerequisite to the total effectiveness of the individual or even a battalion of men. The fighters were in need of a no-nonsense method that could be employed if they became separated from their sword. The rapid growth of ju-jutsu over the feudal period and its subsequent legacy demonstrates how important this particular art was to the warrior classes.

Generally, ju-jutsu techniques are based around the evasion of an attack and how to rapidly defeat the enemy or immobilise them to prevent further attack. There are a variety of ways this can be performed and ju-jutsu teaches very competent techniques. Hand and foot applications are given great respect and so too are the correct ways of how to throw the opponent from an array of positions and angles.

Nowadays, ju-jutsu is taught as an effective means of self-defence to all age groups regardless of gender. There are thousands of devotees in many countries. Original concepts and teachings are in evidence in many martial arts across a broad spectrum. Ju-jutsu has led the way in numerous combat styles.

JUKENDO

Jukendo is a Japanese martial art that is used to describe the way of the bayonet and is the budo development of juken-jutsu. This specific martial art was initially practised in Japanese feudal times. The knowledge of how to use a bayonet was important, especially when faced with an enemy at close-range or when the fighter had exhausted all his ammunition. The art was to gain many students, possibly because this was a regulation and not down to the soldier's discretion.

Juken-jutsu was taught in groups to many soldiers that saw the benefits immediately. The philosophy of jukendo is to duplicate this practice and to preserve the original teachings of it within a non-warring environment. But to retain an element of reality, some jukendo schools include an element of competition between the adherents and teach the art as a sport in much the same way as kendo.

The striking zones are mainly the throat, the lower body and the heart. Each strike is a potential kill or a way of immobilising the enemy. The predetermined strikes were selected for their effectiveness. The rifle is held away from the body and with the two hands. The application is applied by the means of thrusting the rifle and therefore the bayonet in a linear fashion. Straight line fighting is often used, for this allows for more speed and a greater degree of accuracy. The quicker the contestant can strike the target, the better.

To win points a contestant has to demonstrate the precision of the strike and how his target was ultimately exposed. The goal is to hit the opponent in a clear and focused fashion so that the score could not be questioned.

Jukendo has its followers in Japan, although the members are relatively small in number. The sporting side of jukendo has increased its popularity. Obviously, this art was more prominent in the past in times of war when its methods were essential.

KARATE

Karate is without doubt one of the most practiced martial arts in existence today. The name branches from two ideograms, *'kara'* and *'te'*. The first translates into either: empty, Chinese or open and the latter refers to the hand. Thus, we can choose from one of three meanings for karate. The 'Chinese hand' translation is considered archaic by most karate students and those with nationalistic sympathies towards their art's Okinawan roots might even consider it offensive. Possibly the most used phrase to denote this subject is that of 'empty hand', which at face value means a system of unarmed combat. However, if we are to look at the art below its surface we see that there are implications the mind should also be open or empty. With an 'open mind', the student can be free of mental obstacles and in a position to absorb and memorise aspects of their lesson. The Japanese refer to a clear mind as *'mu'*.

Karate is the general name used to describe many schools of strike-based martial arts that are usually Okinawan in origin. They incorporate kicks known as *'geri'*, blocks known as *'uke'*, punches known as *'zuki'* and stances, known as *'dachi'*. Kata is fundamental to karate. The most famous schools of karate are Goju-ryu, Uechi-ryu, Shorin-ryu, Shotokan, Shukokai, Kyokushinkai, Isshin-ryu, Shito-ryu and Wado-ryu, to name but a few.

Karate emphasises the tutelage of kata for all students. Kata, when trained as a solo drill, enable the karateka (a student of karate)

49

to train away from the school and strengthen the precision of their techniques without being closely supervised. All kata have a particular purpose and the principles of the kata are covered by the use of practical analysis known as 'bunkai'. Here, the pupil is shown that the kata can be transformed from a sole person training to how it would effectively work in a practical situation.

The main kata include: Sochin, Niseishi (sometimes referred to as Niju-shiho, Unsu, Chinto often called Gankaku, Sanchin (a principal kata for Goju-ryu), Saifa, Sanseru, Seisan (which is sometimes referred to as Hangetsu), Seipai, Seienchin, Shisochin, Kururunfa, Naihanchi (sometimes referred to as Tekki), Suparumpei, Kushanku (referred to as Kanku), Passai (which is sometimes pronounced and written as Bassai), Wanshu (also known as Enpi), Wankan, Ouseishi (also called Goju-shiho), Jion, Jutte, Ji'in, Lorei (which is also known as Meikyo) and Chinte.

The basics of any karate discipline are known as 'kihon'. Here, the pupil learns the fundamental body mechanics behind techniques. Every school will emphasise the importance and the need for such drills to take place on a regular basis. The pupil's knowledge will stem and grow from a serious approach to the basics.

The stances, or 'dachi', have different shapes, for example 'eko-ashi-dachi' or cat stance, 'kiba-dachi', known as horse or straddle stance, 'fudo-dachi' or fixed stance,' zenkotsu-dachi', which is translated into front leaning stance and so on.

The stance was devised to enable the exponent to move from an attack to a defence with ease and without the karateka losing his balance in doing so. A stance can also be crucial to the power that a person can generate.

The basic kicks are front kick, or *'mae-geri'*, *'mawashi-geri'* or roundhouse kick, *'yoko-geri'*, or side kick and back kick, or *'ushiro-geri'*. From the basic kicks others have been established and included. For example, the jump kick known as *'tobi-geri'* and the crescent kick, which is called *'mikazuki-geri'*. Each kick has a designated area of contact that lessens the chance of injury to the pupil.

Certain karate methods will use traditional training tools to enhance their skill and power. They may use a striking post known as a *'makiwari'*, a weighted jar, or a weighted stick called *'chi-ishi'*, to improve grip. The style of Goju-ryu, which is covered later, places particular emphasis on the use of apparatus such as this.

Most karate involves the use of sparring known as *'kumite'* and prearranged fighting drills. This has led to the creation of Sport Karate, which is a form of competitive fighting inspired by karate. Since the 1960s this has proven very popular in both Japan and the western world. The modern era has seen tournaments, mainly in the USA, move from medals to monetary prizes for the winners and the runners–up. Karate sparring varies from club to club. There has been a recent resurgence in clubs teaching kata-based sparring, which is a non-competitive method that is done full-contact with little to no rules, relying on trust in one's training partner.

Sport Karate is very far removed from reality fighting, but nevertheless is a very popular aspect of karate since its golden era in the 1960s. It is usually semi-contact in nature and often uses a three point scoring system. The exceptions to this rule are Kyokoshinkai Karate, which uses a unique 'Knock down' system, which is full contact. Freestyle Karate is a general term used for a type of semi-contact tournament that uses various ways to score matches. Full-Contact Karate was the result of an experiment between western boxers and karateka to create a sport that would allow more realistic contact. It closely resembles american kickboxing and is essentially the same sport with a few rule changes. Traditional karate tournaments that host Sport Karate bouts also have sections for the performance of kata, which is often judged and scored in a manner comparable to gymnastic or ice-skating displays.

Karate and its schools go from strength to strength throughout the world. Karate is one of the largest martial arts and is one of the most well-known by the man in the street. Most incorporate a grading structure with the use of coloured belts. Traditional uniform or gi are worn. This is a simple tunic and bottoms that are lighter than that used in judo and the more grappling-based arts. As with many Japanese martial arts students are known as 'deshi' and teachers are known as sensei.

Here are some of the most common forms of karate:

Goju-ryu

Goju-ryu is the creation of an Okinawan master by the name of Chojun Miyagi. Miyagi was born in the 1880s and he commenced his early studies of the martial arts with the famous Kanryo Higaonna of Naha-te fame. Miyagi also journeyed to China and studied several combat methods whilst there. He returned home to Naha, establishing his own school in 1917.

Miyagi spent much time developing his own system by drawing knowledge from the various styles he had encountered. The Okinawan master was searching for a discipline that could provide the individual with a comprehensive form of combat that was economic in its methods.

Goju-ryu was eventually to receive its name in 1929. It translates as 'hard/soft school'; to indicate the manner in which attack and defence should be applied. If it is a 'hard' strike then this should receive a 'soft' defence to counter it and vice versa. Hard techniques tend to be those that are direct, whereas soft techniques are generally circular in motion. The original concept is to defeat the strike using an opposing force.

The main kata of Goju-ryu are Gekisai, Saifa, Shisochin, Saiyunchin, Seipai, Seisan, Tensho, Suparunpei, Kururunfa and Sanchin.

There are two major and vitally important types of stance that are stressed by Goju-ryu. They are *'sanchin'* or hourglass stance and *'neko-ashi-dachi'*, or cat stance. Much emphasis is placed on the perfection of these stances, which are taught to the Goju pupil from an early stage, as they make up the art's foundation.

Goju-ryu is a very good example of a karate school that promotes the improvement of the technique by the employment of the traditional training and conditioning implements.

The hand and other parts of the anatomy can be toughened or strengthened to withstand impact. It is not unusual to see masters with skin that has been made hard and abrasive, especially the striking knuckles of the fist. The strength stone is used in a similar manner to a set of weights. The muscles of the wrist and forearms are made more powerful and so too are the fingers in order that the grip can be made more powerful when required. The philosophy is to make the body adaptable and prepared for actual confrontation should it occur.

The breathing exercises, or '*in-ibuki*', are given a high priority in Goju-ryu. The precise manner of exhalation and inhalation can have a major role in most karate styles. More power can certainly be generated with the correct performance

Much time is devoted to the correct mastery of the grip of the hand. Goju-ryu incorporates several throwing and joint-locking applications and strength of grip is seen as fundamental in attaining the right result. Students are given the knowledge of where the nerves and muscle groups are in order that they can be exposed on the foe to bring about a speedy and effective result.

Goju-ryu is classed as being one of the major karate methods in existence today. The style's most well known masters are Eiichi Miyazato, Seiko Higa, Seikichi Toguchi and Meitoku Yagi. Each one went on to create their own school of Goju and gave them a specific name. Miyazato created the Jun-Do-Kan, Higa went on to devise the Kokusai Karate-Kobudo Remnei, Toguchi developed the Shorei Kan and finally Yagi named and developed the Mai-Bu-Kan.

The popularity in part can be attributed to the late and great master Gogen Yamaguchi of the Japanese Goju-kai fame. He was respected throughout the world for his karate expertise and for the spiritual knowledge that he connected to it.

Isshin-Ryu

The founder and father figure of Isshin-ryu was Tatsuo Shimabuku who was born in Okinawa on 19th September 1908. Shimabuku practiced and eventually became one of the top students of Shorin-ryu Karate. In addition to this, he was also an accomplished master of classical weaponry and a student of Goju-ryu Karate. It is also said that he learnt the art of Shaolin-zi from his uncle whilst he was in Fukushu China before he took up karate.

Shimabuku took and researched what he believed to be the strengths of karate and added his own ingredients. Isshin-ryu translates into 'one heart style', a title given by Shimabuku in 1954.

Isshin-ryu has a total of eight kata, seven of which were from already established prearranged sequences. Every kata enables the individual a deeper insight into the origin of this form. The kata of Isshin-ryu are Seiunchin, Seisan, Naihanchi, Wanshu, Sanchin, Chinto, Kusanku and Sunsu.

A distinctive feature of Isshin-ryu is the weapon orientated drills Shimabuku included, such as *'bo-sai-kumite'* or 'staff-trident-fighting'. The possessor of the staff is the aggressor and the trident or pitchfork handler adopts the defensive role of play. Training with weaponry has been seen to enhance the overall self-defence needs of many in today's society.

Being a karate style, Isshin-ryu employs a variety of kicking, punching and blocking techniques. Stance and breathing are given significance and taught to a high tier of knowledge. The techniques that are taught are based on the need for speed and focus.

Isshin-ryu employs a vertical fist in its punching techniques rather than the horizontal method commonly found in most schools of karate. Shimababuku believed it to be a more natural and faster technique. Although not completely unique amongst the Okinawan and mainland Japanese martial arts it seems quite possible Shimababuku got this method from his early days studying in China, where the vertical punch is more commonly taught.

The blocks that are used tend not to apply as much twist in their delivery as other karate styles, but more speed.

Isshin-ryu has gained an enormous following and has many devotees in the United States of America. The American soldiers that were based in Okinawa were exposed to this art and the Americans have been quick to realise the strengths of this karate form, especially in the sparring categories in the tournament circuits. Isshin-ryu, is famed for its fast and versatile movement in an attack or defence mode. Isshin-ryu is said to be one of the major karate styles that exist today.

Shimabuku died in 1975, but he has left a distinct mark on the martial arts. Isshin-ryu has many great instructors that continue to develop the original philosophy.

Kyokushinkai

Kyokushinkai Karate was devised by Choi Young-Li, better known as Masutatsu Oyama, who was born in 1923. This famous Korean master studied fighting systems from his homeland and Chinese kempo before he began training in Gichin Funakoshi's Shotokan Karate, gaining a 4th Dan black belt by the time he was twenty-four. He also trained in boxing, judo and, under the guidance of the Korean master So Nei Chu, he studied Goju-ryu Karate. He built a reputation for being a very courageous fighter and greatly impressed those who observed his many combat skills.

Oyama was to create an even larger status with his many exploits and adventures that astonished martial artists and laymen alike. Oyama was not content or overly impressed with the effectiveness of the martial arts he had encountered. With such a desire to acquire more competent fighting methods he decided to venture to the United States of America to cross the continental divides. Whilst in America, he challenged wrestlers and boxers to fights, to test what he had already learnt and to gain an insight into their combat drills.

Clearly, he was prepared to put his strength, agility and resolve to the ultimate test. Oyama's drive was to fight numerous opponents and he displayed no fear, but total confidence in himself.

Having fought all that met the challenge, Oyama decided to pit his wits and knowledge against fifty-two bulls. Three bulls were killed instantly with a series of hand techniques and he claimed the horns of forty-nine using 'knife-hand' (edge of the hand strikes). This attained him a legendary status. He had surely faced a life or death situation and become victorious on every occasion much to the delight of the audience.

In 1956, Masutatsu Oyama finally gave a title to his method of combat. He selected Kyokushinkai which appropriately translates into 'the ultimate truth style'. Kyokushinkai has gathered many thousands of pupils throughout the world, largely because of the high standards that are set and the reputation of its founder.

Oyama adapted the special characteristics of his chosen methods and he eventually was to create what he believed to be the most combat-oriented and most effective of all martial arts. In its early life the style had given an emphasis and a significant role to kata. The Kyokushinkai kata are largely of a Goju-ryu and Shotokan decent.

Oyama's method established 'knock down' sparring, unlike other schools of karate, which prefer to see less contact being made. Kyokushinkai contains what is known as the 'one hundred man kumite', where a master eventually faces one hundred opponents in succession. Only a small elite set of masters have performed such a feat.

Kyokushinkai has created a great reputation amid the martial arts as a whole. It has built a following that has made it one of the most popular karate schools that are in existence today.

Sankukai

Sankukai is a karate method that has attracted many devotees over recent years. This martial art was founded and pioneered by Yoshinao Nanbu. He had originally been a student of the famed shukokai school of karate until he parted company from it to research his own themes and ideologies. Nanbu never forgot the teachings that he had received and had mastered. He was a great master and innovator and sought to establish his own specific field.

Nanbu was to establish a method of karate that was successfully transported throughout the globe, largely due to the respect that he and his ways had achieved.

Sankukai is similar to most karate disciplines, in that the students undergo a specialised study of how to punch, block and kick, whilst learning how to perform kata. Sankukai has a very popular sporting side and is often chosen for this aspect. However, despite much of the art being geared towards competition it still retains many traditional values.

Nanbu introduced joint-locks and sweeps from his own experiences to improve his teaching of Karate. He had spent time investigating which techniques would be apt and could be readily taught in his syllabus. He believed that other martial forms had aspects or features that he could adopt into his teachings, and introduced his own ideals to the total teaching package. The students would acquire knowledge of many aspects of combat and be well taught in their various components.

Other establishments have introduced weaponry, for example, the 'sai' and the 'bo', or trident and the staff respectively. The choice of weapons will depend on the skills that the teacher may have learnt from another source. There are no standardised weapons but the ancient tools of war and farming have enlightened many pupils and their overall fighting comprehension and general understanding. It is a karate method that is open-minded; Nanbu deliberately left the door ajar for amendments to be made.

Sankukai has managed to attract many great masters, which has served to further improve the skills of the instructors at large. Sankukai continues to go from strength to strength.

Shito-ryu

Shito-ryu was created and promoted by Kenwa Mabuni, born in 1889 in Okinawa, who began his path in the martial arts at the tender age of thirteen. Mabuni was considered an unhealthy child but he started out by enrolling and being accepted by Master Ankoh Itosu, and he never missed a day of training until he was twenty. Mabuni then trained in the Shurite system under the supervision of Master Kanryo Higashionna of Naha. It is said that he favoured the Chinese White Crane methods and was inspired by kobu-jutsu under the guidance of Yabiku and Aragaki. Mabuni had taken it upon himself to study several different fighting forms and gained his early knowledge from great masters across a wide spectrum.

The name of this school of karate was taken from the first characters of 'itosu' (Shi) and 'Higashionna' (To). Mabuni travelled to Japan in the late 1920s and first found a home in Tokyo, following a path of another Okinawan master Gichin Funakoshi, and later moved to Osaka in south-west Japan.

Mabuni was in an unrivalled position of being able to teach many forms of kata. The quantity of kata is greater than any other Karate system. Shito-ryu has taken them to new heights in terms of the numbers that are readily available.

As well as unarmed applications, Mabuni had a tendency towards weaponry and gave demonstrations of his mastery for all to see. He had promoted all the schools of combat that he had encountered and he had been an enthusiastic teacher for them all, whether they were unarmed or connected to the weapon systems.

Balance and posture are key features of this martial art form. Shito-ryu highlights strong links between the individual's stance and the manner in which a particular technique is performed.

There is a requirement for speed and accuracy of delivery and execution of an application, whatever that may be. The basics, or 'kihon', are fundamental and taught at every stage of the student's progression through the ranking structure. The founder emphasised the need for regular practice and determination to succeed, and the need to be prepared to react quickly.

Mabuni was a pioneer of karate and the branches of Shito-ryu and allied families include, Kanei Mabuni and Manzo Iwata's Shitokai system, Takamasa Tomoyori's school of Kenyu-kai, Yuki Mori Kuniba's system of Seishin kai and Masaru Watanabe's form known as Seiki-kai. The creator of Shito-ryu was indeed to have a great influence until his death in 1952. Kenwa Mabuni had left a great legacy of an ideology that will remain strong long into the future.

Shorin-ryu

The Okinawan towns of Shuri and Tomari are instrumental in the establishment of Shorin-ryu and Shorei-ryu karate. This school has nurtured many popular karate forms. The Shorin-ryu can claim it was the forerunner of the more widely practised karate methods that exist today.

The Shorin-ryu teaches the students the correct technique of kicking, or '*geri-waza*'. The kicks can be either frontal, roundhouse, side or reverse in their nature. Shorin-ryu considers kicks that are below the belt as more important. The Shorin-ryu masters believed that high-level kicks could be a disadvantage as there is a larger region of the body to protect and therefore exposed to attack.

The unarmed teachings are supplemented with the Okinawan weapon art of kobudo. Certain instructors elect to bring traditional weaponry such as the staff and bladed weaponry into their curriculum and specialise in doing so. The '*nunchaku*' or flail, the '*tonfa*' or handle, the '*kama*' known as a sickle and the *sai* or trident may also be chosen as an implement to be taught to the class members, or a mixture of them.

The principal masters of the Shorin-ryu include Yasutsune Itosu, Kentsu Yabu, Chotoku Kyan, Chosin Chibana and Soken Matsumura. Shorin-ryu has been blessed with some great scholars and masters that have all left a mark on this martial art and the other allied disciplines that have branched from it.

Shotokan

Shotokan karate was founded by an Okinawan martial artist called Gichin Funakoshi who was born in the village of Shuri in 1868. He received an early education in the martial arts from two Okinawan masters, Azato and Itosu. It was noted that Funakoshi was an enthusiastic and determined student.

Funakoshi's father was a low ranking official of the samurai class, known as a '*Shizoku*', and eventually the talented Karateka was to be introduced to more and more masters of Okinawan systems. He became a devoted scholar, usually learning the crafts in isolation and total secrecy. He was to be one of the main pioneers, transporting the Okinawan unarmed methods to the Japanese mainland in the early 1920s.

Shotokan is a karate discipline that gained its name from Funakoshi's pen name of Shoto, and the training hall, known as a *'kan'*. The school is founded on deep stance and the ability to generate power from this posture. The Shotokan establishment uses a tiger as its emblem.

This system has many kata, including Taikokyu, Kihon, Heian, Tekki, Bassai, Kanku, Hangetsu, Enpi, Ji'in, Jion, Jitte, Unsu, Meikyo, Sochin, Niju-shiho, Goju-shiho, Chinte, Gankaku, Wankan. The Heian kata, which number one to five in sequence, and translate into 'tranquil mind', are usually the first kata that are taught alongside the basic kata of Taikokyu and Kihon.

Tekki, which means 'horse-riding', has a set of three sequences in total. Bassai, 'penetrating a fortress', and Kanku, or 'looking at the sky', have two sets of sequences each. The order that the kata are taught to the students is normally at the instructor or association's discretion.

In 1921, the Japanese Crown Prince visited the shores of Okinawa to witness an exhibition of karate. Gichin Funakoshi was one of the organisers and he, along with other Okinawan masters, put on a show. After several demonstrations of the methods that he had acquired, he was invited to display the art, which he and others did at the Great Hall of Shuri Castle. The Young Crown Prince of Japan was to be in attendance and he was so impressed with the demonstration that he formally invited Gichin and others to perform on the Japanese mainland in front of his own martial art masters. Eventually, the founder of judo, Jigaro Kano, was to request a special showing of the fighting skills, which Gichin did, though reluctantly at first.

One must note that at this period of Japanese history there was a bitter hatred towards anything that was Chinese. The nations were sworn enemies. The original name for karate was *'t'ang hand'* which was sometimes thought to refer to a Chinese origin. The name was quickly amended to what it is now known as today.

Eventually Funakoshi Gichin was to acquire many followers of his method. He eventually took residence in mainland Japan and opened a school. Other masters from Okinawa were quick to follow suit and the Japanese islands saw some of the finest masters that have ever existed and probably ever will. Here, the foundations had been laid, and they have been successfully built on ever since.

After the Second World War the helm of the Shotokan was passed to the Japanese Karate Association. Gichin Funakoshi believed that his age was a burden to the promotion and the further development of his method. The running of the Japanese Karate Association was left to selected masters, for example, Masatoshi Nakayama, Shigeru Egami and Isao Obata.

However, there are also many excellent Shotokan instructors who operate outside and are not connected to the Japanese Karate Association. In 1957, Gichin Funakoshi died and many of his loyal high graded students were to form splinter groups from the Japanese Karate Association. Masatoshi Nakayama was left to conduct the affairs and the promotion of the Japanese Karate Association.

Shotokan has an enormous following and a massive membership across the continents. The art has been blessed and fortunate to have some charismatic instructors and respected master grades that have assisted in the systems growth over the last few decades.

Shukokai

The Shukokai martial art system is a typical Karate discipline. The founder of the Shukokai School was Chojiro Tani, who was initially a scholar in the Shito-ryu establishment, which he particularly liked and admired. Tani was to achieve a high recognition within the school and found he had gained his own admirers.

Chojiro Tani was interested in the sporting aspects of the martial arts. He believed that a fighting system should encourage practice and sparring. Tani was a believer in enabling the student to gain a deeper understanding of how their skills could be employed and feel the results for themselves. With this understanding in mind, he commenced his own individual experimentation. He wanted a mechanism that would attract those of a similar ideology and who could assist in his studies.

Chojiro Tani was to devote much time and effort to pursuing his goals before he actually gave his concept the name of Shukokai, which translates into 'way for all'. The stances are relatively high, thus giving the student mobility and the benefits of speed and the alteration of posture and movement.

Shukokai favours rapid kicking and punching methods that can be performed easily from a constantly changing stance should the need arise. There is an array of kicking and punching styles to choose from that permits the student to have a versatile approach during free practice and competition. The blocks have been simplified to promote the general effectiveness of the student in a tournament scenario or in a street confrontation. The student is versed in how to evade an intended strike and how to counter accordingly whilst remaining on guard.

Shukokai is also noted for its modern and scientific research into developing power in its strikes. Sigeru Kimura, one of the founder's most devoted students, spent his entire life looking into the most practical and logical ways of delivering force. One of his conclusions was that the hip should always be brought forward before a hand strike is delivered and, contrary to the way many systems teach, not at the same time. Shukokai uses a unique impact pad to test such principles. It is often mimicked by putting two swimming floats together and holding them between the chest and stomach.

This school of karate still holds on to the traditional virtues as well as the sporting side. Etiquette and respect is of the most paramount importance. The system will continually propagate the initial teachings. The defence of the student is important and the manner in which the person conducts him or herself, for instance, to hard work and dedication is a prerequisite of the art.

Shukokai has a massive membership. Chojiro Tani has produced many respected masters that have enforced his original theories.

Uechi-Ryu

Uechi-ryu karate was founded by the great Okinawan karate master, Kanbun Uechi. Uechi began training in martial arts in the Chinese Fukien Province, where he trained in the Crane, Dragon and Tiger boxing styles.

Kanbun Uechi had the drive and determination to labour many hours and strive to understand the meanings and purposes of the Chinese forms. He was an enthusiastic scholar and attentive student. He was to remain in China for over a decade in the search for enlightenment and to realise his dreams of gaining a deeper understanding and practical approach to fighting.

The Uechi-ryu system is closely connected to the Naha-te form. Kanbun Uechi was a firm believer in the power and the strength that can be attained by implementing a meaningful and well-balanced stance and firm posture.

Additionally, Uechi promoted the use of the correct ways to inhale and exhale, depending on the technique that is to be employed at any one given moment. Speed and split second timing are also covered and trained on a regular basis. The objective is to train the mind as well as the body. The art demonstrates the virtues and the strengths of uniting the mind and the body in harmony.

Uechi-ryu was only to originally have taken on board three types of kata, however over the years this has increased and those that are generally taught and learnt include: Sanchin, Konshu, Seichin, Seiru, Seisan, Kanchin, Sanseiryu and others, depending on the instructor.

Wado-Ryu

The karate style of Wado-ryu was the creation of Hironori Ohtsuka who was born in the 1890s. It is one of the major styles of karate that exists today and has thousands of adherents throughout the world and many great masters have developed from the original teachings.

Ohtsuka began his martial arts training in ju-jutsu, in particular that of the Shin-do Yoshin-ryu style. At the age of thirty he was awarded the title of grandmaster in 1928. In the same year at the age of thirty he commenced his education in karate under the guidance of Gichin Funakoshi and quickly became one his assistant instructors. In addition to studying under Funakoshi he studied under Choki Motobu and Mabuni. Wado-ryu was registered in around 1939 and translates as 'way of peace'.

Wado-ryu puts an emphasis on body- shifting and avoidance. The objective is to cause pain and injury to the opponent, whilst restricting any possible injury to the karateka. This type of body-striking and the knowledge of where and how to strike is known as atemi-jutsu, as described earlier. There are over three hundred regions of the anatomy that can be struck or twisted that will inflict damage or the immobilisation of the adversary. Hironori Ohtsuka, who was also a professional bonesetter, was noted for his exceptional knowledge of atemi-jutsu.

The studies that Ohtsuka had undergone in ju-jutsu were to pay dividends. He systematically added certain joint-locking techniques and choking methods to his style of karate. He believed, as many others do, that the goal was to provide a comprehensive means of self-defence.

Wado-ryu instructs the need for both speed and flexibility of the mind and the body. Wado stylists use a high stance to aid mobility and speed. The aspect of free sparring, known as 'kumite', is given a great deal of emphasis and many dojos have taken to sport.

Wado-ryu features the use of the following kata: Pinan of which there are a series of five, Naihanchi, Kushanku, Seishan, Chinto, Wanshu, Passai, Jitte, Jion, Rohai and Niseishi. The way those that are taught will be at the instructor's discretion, similar to other forms of karate and will be reliant on the syllabus concerned. The kata can be used as a tool in the tournament arenas and also be an ingredient of a grading examination. Kata give the disciple the teachings of how specific techniques and applications should be performed when they practise in isolation or when removed from the class and instruction environment.

KEMPO

Kempo is a Japanese word that means 'way of the fist'. The equivalent to this term in Chinese is *'ch'uan fa'* and in the Cantonese language it is known as *'ken fat'*.

The 'way of the fist' is a collective name for numerous extractions of the martial art and science that involves logical hand and leg techniques. Applications of attack and defence are taught and the students are encouraged to research their own individual ideas to increase the competence of the form. The masters are versed in how to exploit the weaknesses of the opponent, whether in armed or unarmed confrontations. Specific schools will teach hand strikes and kicks and incorporate joint-locks, nerve-strikes and throwing-drills into their system.

There are many sources and establishments that affiliate to the name of kempo, or the Chinese equivalent. The art covers a large assortment of practical systems and some attach spiritual awareness to the overall philosophy.

There are visible differences between the kempo establishments that started in Japan and in China. The main separation is how emphasis is placed on kicking and the ways that a stance is adopted. Some prefer to encourage low-level kicks that are viewed as being less vulnerable, the student reducing the potential of being hit because their body is more compact and therefore easier to cover with their own blocks. The stance and posture can vary in length from one school to another. There are those that prefer to adopt a high stance, where the legs are closer together, again for the benefit of being more compact. The stance is important to all martial artists as it assists movement or evasion from one position to the next. The stance used will additionally play a significant role in determining the student's balance and the power that can be generated. Different styles will have varying opinions on certain stances and also to application of hip rotation, which is paramount to the execution of a good hand strike or kick.

It is believed that the history of kempo can be followed back through thousands of years. Some state that this martial art can be seen in Bodhidharma's 'eighteen positions' around 5 AD, making it one of the most ancient of all documented forms of combat.

KENDO

Kendo is a modern martial method that derives from ken-jutsu. Kendo, which means 'way of the sword', is a Japanese form of fencing for sport and spiritual pursuits in line with the budo movement of martial arts, whereas ken-jutsu, or 'art of the sword', is the ancient system of fighting with live blades for survival. One needs to understand both to gain a better overall concept of Japanese fencing. Kendo was established into two main types: battle-orientated kendo, which had the sole philosophy of defeating the enemy, and school kendo, which had the aim of refining and perfecting kendo technique.

Armed uprisings against the Japanese government in the 1870s, promoted interest in swordsmanship. In 1879 the Tokyo Police Force instigated a course in kendo. There was a national need for the fighting skills and defensive crafts that could be acquired from studying this particular martial art form. The Sino-Japanese war of 1894–95 and the Russo-Japanese war of 1904–05 both served to further enhance this desire to increase the population's awareness and thirst to acquire knowledge of this art. Kendo became part of the Japanese school curriculum in 1911.

Kendo students use a simulated sword that is made from bamboo and known as a 'shinai'. The shinai is made of four pieces of flexible bamboo and the hilt is known as a 'tsuba'. Other replacements for the Japanese sword have also been used, such as a blunt metal sword, known as an '*iaito*', or a sword made out of a single piece of wood, called a '*bokken*', but they are not safe enough for active competition. In fact, the legendary samurai Myomoto Musashi used the *bokken* as an effective duelling weapon.

The sport of kendo enforces that the kendoka (student or practitioner of kendo) wears protective equipment to further reduce the potential of injury. The armour is given specific terms. For example, the wrist gloves are called '*kote*', the body or breastplate is known as '*do*', the stomach and abdomen guard is called '*tare*', and the face and head-guard is known as '*men*'. This equipment was developed in the eighteenth century and the modern armour has remained very similar to this early design.

Classical ceremony and dress are important features of this modern martial sport.

The student wears traditional Japanese dress; the jacket is called a '*keiko-gi*' and a divided skirt is worn that is known as a *hakama*.

The objective of kendo is to strike the opponent with formalised moves at areas of their anatomy. The body targets, called '*datotsui*', include the left wrist or '*hidari kote*', the right wrist or '*migi kote*', and the centre of the head or '*shomen*', the left and right side of the head or '*hidari*' and '*migi men*' respectively, the left and right side of the ribcage or '*hidari*' and '*migi do*' respectively, the throat or '*nodo*' and the chest known as '*mune*'. All targets are seen as areas that would either kill or maim the enemy should a real weapon be used.

The *shinai* is held with both hands and the actual cutting action should be performed with the full extension of the arms. A '*kiai*', or spirit shouting, accompanies the strike. Kendo has a strong basis in spiritual and mental doctrines, which should never be separated when learning the art.

As with a large number of the martial arts listed here, the Japanese warrior classes are strongly attached to the study and history of this martial art. Some modern-day kendoka perceive practising this art, which is uniquely rooted in the past, as an opportunity to understand the mentality of a specific era. The Japanese were, and still are, strong believers in the respect that should be observed towards their ancestors, something that is seen in the Shinto religion and philosophy.

Tournaments are held on a regular basis and culminate in multinational competitions; such is the membership connected to this sport. Kendo has an enormous following in Japan today. Probably the expense of the equipment and the necessary kit has held back the membership in other parts of the globe. However, many fine establishments do exist if one cares to look hard enough.

KEN-JUTSU

Ken-jutsu, or 'art of the sword', is a classical form of Japanese swordsmanship. The art has a long tradition of values that preserve the code of conduct for master and student alike.

Ken-jutsu was one of the primary sources of a combat education given to the Japanese feudal warrior. As the name suggests, the art of the sword is how to use the weapon and where to strike to acquire maximum results in conflict. The methodology was easily absorbed into their regime, as there was a need to understand how best to kill the opponent in the quickest way possible. The sword was a principle tool of the warrior and the size and weight was at the discretion of the owner.

The Japanese are renowned for their construction of swords. The blade is tempered in a special way that is rarely seen in other countries. Samurai were known to wear more than one sword of varying lengths. Some schools, most famously Myomoto Musashi's dojo, perfected the art of using two swords simultaneously.

The 'daito', or long sword, measures longer than two 'shaku' (one *shaku* is 11.9 inches). The '*wakizashi*' is the most common type of short sword, measuring between one and two *shaku*. It is also sometimes given the non-specific term of '*kodach*'. The *tanto* measures less than one *shaku* and is a type of dagger. Styles varied for different reasons over the feudal eras and produced many different swords. The 'katana' is the most common style of Japanese sword seen today. It is often believed that the katana was developed from the longer more curved cavalry sword known as a 'taichi'. Most Japanese swords are curved in design, but this was not always the case. The 'ken' or 'chokuto' was a straight sword used in earlier times. Its design was said to influence the modern-day development of Korean sword arts.

Each fighter would have their own manner of carrying the weapon but they were normally strapped to the back. This permitted the drawing of the weapon and gave the warrior a selection of cutting angles to choose from. The speed at which the sword could be drawn was significant to where it was placed. It was and still is the norm to hold the weapon with both hands and to fully extend the arms when performing a cutting motion. The notion was not to stop at the point of contact but to cut straight through the target. It was common to see the warrior attempt to completely cut the opponent in half or take off his head. Japanese swordsmanship was famous throughout the world and often the enemy was frightened before the battle had begun.

As mentioned earlier, the warrior would adhere to strict codes that would ordinarily control their lives. This was the 'warrior way', known as bushido, and the warriors themselves were known as bushi. The protection of one's family and allegiance to a certain family or set of individuals, known as daimyo, was his priority. Each daimyo would have a father figure that the warriors would risk their lives for without question. Many a feud over land and possession would result in numerous battles between different families. Ken-jutsu was seen as a necessary skill to assist in ensuring a good future for one's family and daimyo.

Today ken-jutsu is taught by the means of kata. The kata have been devised to assist in the accurate lunges and swings of the sword, in both attack and defence. The science of this martial art is awe inspiring in itself. Masters are keen to demonstrate the skills of their trade and have captivated audiences with their speed and precision.

A wooden practice sword, known as a *bokken*, now often replaces the actual sword. Ken-jutsu is the forerunner of modern day kendo.

KYUDO

Kyudo, literally 'the way of the bow', is the modern science and study of Japanese archery. Kyudo is the budo follow-on from kyu-jutsu. After firearms replaced the longbow, archery became a recreational and sporting pursuit. The name kyudo, however, only became widespread after the American occupation of Japan from 1945 to 1952, when the practice of martial arts for the battlefield was banned.

This martial art is based around the practice and philosophy that is attached to the drawing and the eventual firing of the arrow. A longbow, known as a '*yumi*', is employed and there are three basic lengths of the arrow, known as '*mato*': the fourteen inch target, the thirty-two inch target and the sixty-four inch target.

Kyudoka (kyudo students) seek to obtain perfect scores for precision in firing arrows and in their understanding of the religious significance of the weapon. Like most traditional Japanese budo, spiritual and mental attributes are as important as physical ability. It is said that the individual who applies all these virtues is a complete fighting machine.

Each bow is methodically crafted to the owner's requirements and needs. The bearer has the option to select the length and the weight of their bow. Modern day bows usually have a carbon body, but little has changed in terms of design since the twelfth century.

Weights vary from under thirteen kilograms to forty-two kilograms (the most powerful recorded bow). The Japanese bow is one of the longest in the world with accordingly very long arrows. Unlike other systems of archery when the arrow is fully drawn the tail end stretches behind the archer's ear. Mastery of the art necessitates a lot of time and devotion. A typical session would see twenty to forty arrows fired, which can be quite a strenuous activity, but pales to the hundred or so that would have been fired when the art was geared towards the battlefield and known as kyu-jutsu.

The foundation of kyudo is to respect the weapon and appreciate that it is a lethal art. Training is done under strict supervision. Kyudo is an attempt to recreate kyu-jutsu and understand the importance that was placed on the archer in the battlefield. It permits all ages and genders to practise together. The manner in

which the student adopts the stance is important for it allows the individual to have balance and to absorb the recoil after firing. Breathing and posture are also covered in great detail.

The Zen Nihon Kyudo Federation was established in 1953. Kyudo has many disciples in Japan and very few in the rest of the world. Japanese traditional culture displays respect for all things that have held an important place in their many wars and battles, and kyudo inspires that passion. The pupils wear traditional dress and observe a code of conduct that the instructor lays down from day one.

KYU-JUTSU

Kyu-jutsu, or 'art of the bow', commenced around 800 AD with the promotion of Yoshiie Minamoto. He was a high status samurai and was the Chief of the Army. It was a very much taught and sought after martial art throughout the feudal times of Japan. The archer played a substantial part in the victory or otherwise of a battle. Kyu-jutsu was a martial art that required great skill and the masters of it were worth their weight in gold. Armies demanded the very best from their archers since they would normally commence the battles.

The bow and arrow has historically been proven to be an extremely effective weapon and defence in open ground would be nearly impossible. Even warriors on horseback were at a major risk from the skilled bowman. The results of wars have often been in the hands of the archers, and not simply in the Japanese islands. Perhaps the best comparison in the west was the success of English archers during the Hundred Years War when they defeated the supposed superior technology of the French crossbow.

The bow is a light weapon and this makes it easy for the archer to transport from one location to another. The weapon could be made at little cost but that of the time of the craftsman, who became important themselves. A bow has a large range of fire and the targets can be picked out with ease, depending on the ability of the archer. This enables an army to be cut down in numbers before eye-to-eye confrontation takes place. This meant even women and children could be used as archers, as they could leave the scene before hand-to-hand combat could take place.

Often the archers used their skills along with the art of the sword to enhance their overall combat competence and were valued by their generals or their family chieftains. It meant that they could fight at both short and long range. A warrior's status was linked to the skills that he could bring to an army.

After the introduction of firearms and allied explosives to Japan, kyu-jutsu all but died out. Honda Toshizane is often regarded as the saviour of Japanese archery for his creation of the Honda-ryu, where he combined elements of the warrior style with the ceremonial court style. This was really the birthplace for modern kyudo.

NAGINATADO

Naginatado, or 'way of the reaping (or long) sword', is a martial art form that has successfully passed the test of time. This martial art form is the modern development of the war-like 'Naginata-jutsu'.

A *'naginata'* is a type of Japanese weapon similar to the European halberd or glaive, comprising of a long wooden pole or staff with a long curved sword-like blade at the end. The average length of the weapon is approximately seven feet, but the measurement can slightly deviate depending on the student's preference. The weapon's length can make it cumbersome and awkward to use to begin with. Yet, in the hands of a skilled practitioner this deadly form looks graceful and far removed from its original purpose. Today, for practice reasons, solid wood and bamboo equivalents, measuring approximately two feet in length, have replaced the blade.

There are two types of naginatado taught today, classical and modern, known as 'Atarashi Naginatado'. Both share the budo ethic of combining physical endeavours with the development of personal spirituality and character, and both follow the traditional systemised sequence of strikes, cuts and thrusts. Students are taught how best to gain the correct strike from this long weapon. The ability of the individual is measured on the performance that he or she displays.

Atarashi Naginatado's main distinction from the classical form is its sporting or tournament element. There are many competitions held throughout the year in Japan. The points are scored on the accuracy of attaining the predetermined targets in similar manner to kendo, using a bamboo *naginata*. For safety reasons, the participants wear protective armour, similar to what kendo students wear. There is also an additional piece of equipment called a *'suneate'*, or shin-guard, as strikes are permitted to lower parts of the legs. The protective kit is important, as injuries would be frequent if not observed correctly.

The targets that are used in naginatado are the shin, the head, the forearms and the torso. The striking areas have been selected for their effectiveness on the battlefield. Each target would either kill or immobilise the enemy. The design of the blade allows these effective strikes to be performed and registered against the opponent. The shape of the blade is curved and permits reaping or slashing cuts to be displayed and each carries a score or point. The weapon is best employed using circular or sweeping actions. The striking action and the speed depend on the ability or the level the student has attained.

Naginatado is somewhat contained within the Japanese islands, where it has a large following of men and women and the students are taken from an early age. Of the estimated eighty thousand practitioners of naginatado, most participate in Atarashi Naginata.

NAGINATA-JUTSU

Naginata-jutsu, or 'art of the reaping (or long) sword', features heavily in Japanese military history. The *naginata*, as used in naginatado, is a spear with a curved blade attached at one end. The curve enables the user to cut in swinging movements and the targets can be numerous. Naginata-jutsu flourished in the feudal periods of the Japanese islands and many ancient paintings have depicted the effectiveness of such a weapon. The samurai saw the potential for such a weapon at long-range.

It could be used to attack or repel a sword-wielding enemy, or against another *naginata* carrier. Naginata-jutsu was also a favourite method of killing a warrior who may have been on horseback, as the rider could be reached quite easily and effectively with this long-range weapon. The *naginata* was often used in conjunction with other weapons. A common strategy was to use the length of the *naginata* to make the first strike before the sword delivered the secondary strike. The *naginata* is principally applied in a swinging action, but with the correct motion it can also be used to thrust at the opponent.

Naginata-jutsu was taught to the average warrior. The weapon could be made quite cheaply and many skilled tradesmen could construct them. A *naginata* became a dominant feature in times of war and clan disputes, often deciding the outcome of a battle. The versatility of this weapon required plenty of practice and an understanding of how the weapon could be best used in the circumstances.

NAGINATA-JUTSU

Naginata-jutsu suffered a decline with the introduction of firearms and the system is studied today via the established naginatado schools in Japan. This martial art has largely remained in its homeland, but it should not be overlooked as it had a major role in the martial arts as a whole.

NIN-JUTSU

The 'ninja' were originally hired spies and skilled assassins that plied their trade in feudal Japan. The particular martial art of the ninja was and still is known as nin-jutsu.

This martial art has been the subject of controversy and even mockery by those who do not really understand it. Numerous discussions and arguments emerge from people who have little or no knowledge of the style, except for what they have seen in films depicting super-human characteristics, or read in unreliable sources.

In reality the ninja did exist and their abilities are documented in certain texts. The many tales and yarns should not be entangled in the truth. Unfortunately, myths and legends will always surround this martial art. Nin-jutsu was a well-concealed form that was deliberately taught in isolation. The art encompassed many different disciplines with the aim of creating a perfect fighting individual or an assassin.

Nin-jutsu was chiefly taught between the thirteenth and seventeenth centuries AD. The 'art of invisibility', nin-jutsu was well known in the Iga and Koga regions of Japan, where the masters were particularly famed. Other establishments were dotted around the Japanese islands, but none were considered as effective.

A potential student of nin-jutsu was normally taken at an early age in order that the many skills could be passed on before they were of a warrior age. The ninja were taught the uses and application of many weapons that included the sword, the knife, the spear, the bow and arrow, the blowpipe, darts and knuckle-dusters. The variety of the student's arsenal was a necessity, as different situations would call for different arms.

Deception and evasion appear to be key features when one discusses the ninja. For example, a distraction could be created by smoke bombs or fires could be deliberately started to draw the enemy's attention away. Any incident that could help would be used to cause panic and confusion, two things that aided the purpose of the ninja. Manufactured incidents, large or small, could give the time needed to perform their tasks. A specialist evasion method that was taught to many students was '*nawanuke-no-jutsu*'. Here the ninja was versed on how to dislocate their own joints in order to escape bonds or ropes after capture.

Weaponry was an important feature of the training package. Life or death depended on their talent and the teachings were as practical as possible. Certain military operations may have necessitated the performance of the ninja and therefore their success was of the most paramount importance. As well as the orthodox weapons, for instance the sword and dagger, the ninja also carried, when deemed appropriate, a short bow called a '*hankyu*' and grenades known as '*nage teppo*'. Additionally, they were skilled with a blowpipe that fired poisonous darts and pins. Needle blowing, called '*fuki bari*', was a lethal example of how stealth and the element of surprise were utilised by these shadow warriors.

When travelling to a venue the ninja would wear clothing that would camouflage them. Black clothing would be worn at night and green if they were to travel across fields. The ninja were also expected to be masters of disguise in order that they could move without arousing suspicion and avoid detection. Several disguises were used such as a travelling actor or *'sarugaku'*, a mountain priest or *'yamabushi'*, a merchant or *'akindo'*, a farmer or *'tsunegata'*, and a Buddhist priest or *'sukke'*.

Nin-jutsu were taught how to create poisons and other deadly concoctions to kill the enemy. In addition to having a grounding in how to make such poisons from leaves and berries, they also made and carried their own medicine known as *'kusuri'*. We can see that there were many aspects of knowledge that the student had to learn and would be required to perform as a successful martial artist.

Today, there are very few acclaimed masters of nin-jutsu. The most well-known and respected is the Togakure-ryu.

NIPPON KEMPO

The founder of the Japanese martial art known as nippon kempo was Masuru Sawayama. Sawayama created this fighting system from the experience he had gained of the different forms he had studied. He had served to become a master grade in the martial arts and had a deep understanding of the workings of others. He built a reputation as someone who would work hard to reach the goals that he had set himself. nippon kempo developed after much research in the 1930s and served as a tribute to the desires and enthusiasm that the founder had clearly demonstrated.

Nippon kempo is founded around the sparring or free fighting ways and methods. At its heart it is a sport, but does contain traditional customs and ethics and some schools teach self-defence. All students are given a sound education and understanding of the anatomy and where and how to strike. The ideal is to give the student a practical basis of how this method would function in a real life scenario. Sawayama was determined to provide the principles of reality in his own training and teaching.

Nippon kempo attempts to recreate reality combat in a safe environment. All students wear protective equipment to reduce the chance of injury. Protective helmets, gloves and body-protectors are adorned in order that full contact strikes can be utilised where possible. The armour is supposed to be based upon that worn by the feudal samurai. All protective equipment needs to be able to sustain and absorb a great deal of impact whilst at the same time be comfortable.

The exponent is taught how to strike and kick correctly with speed being a major component. Through constant practice and time afforded to the study, the individual begins to understand what their capabilities are and what they may need to work harder at. By creating a real fighting environment, the student becomes aware of how to control their strikes and when best to apply them. There is little need for self-control.

Students are encouraged to alternate their sparring partners. By doing this the student will learn how to deal with smaller or taller opponents that will have different levels of power and reach. The ways of evasion and the correct blocking procedures are covered and form an elaborate web of defensive prowess.

With the use of constant training, the student realises the importance of balance and the correct way to defend themselves as well as attack. Consequently, respect for the opponent is an important component of nippon kempo.

The curriculum and sport is based around comprehensive unarmed combat and even features ground fighting. nippon kempo has a large membership and following in Japan, where it has largely remained, although there are also associations in the United Kingdom, the USA and in Europe. nippon kempo commands a high respect throughout the Japanese islands, which has helped the form to flourish and gain many noted masters.

SHORINJI KEMPO

Shorinji kempo is a Japanese interpretation of the Shaolin Temple's code of boxing and fighting disciplines. Michiomi Nakano, who is probably better known as Doshin So, introduced these Chinese disciplines to the Japanese islands in the 1940s. The founder made his way to China during the Second World War, where he learnt several systems from noted Chinese martial art teachers. These Chinese forms were to have a profound result on the rest of his life and the path of the fighting forms that he was eventually to master and teach.

In addition to this, Doshin So was to study ju-jutsu under the Hakko-ryu and received directed guidance from Yoshiharu Okuyama. He would blend these Chinese and Japanese styles to create a hybrid that was to satisfy his personal interpretations of how a comprehensive fighting discipline should look.

Shorinji kempo was created at the end of World War II after Doshin So bore witness to a nation crippled by defeat. He was inspired to use his martial teachings to bring self-esteem and harmony back to his countrymen. Shorinji kempo has a strong connection to a spiritual awareness; a mental approach is significant in the composition of a martial art. Shorinji kempo is centred on Kongo Zen and promotes these ideologies within the system. In fact, it began as a religious order, but swiftly became adopted as a 'way'. Doshin So took it upon himself to train the youth of Japan, the country's future, to have strong bodies, indomitable spirits, a harmonious philosophy and focused minds.

With a wealth of knowledge at its core, this martial art contains punching and kicking systems as well as blocks and evasion techniques. The kicks and punches are known as '*goho*' and the throws and grappling methods are called '*juho*'. The master grades usually wear Buddhist monk clothing that is called *hoi*. The kicks are used to engage the opponent at long-range with the hand strikes either following the kicks or being used to repel the attacker at close-range. The student is educated in the numerous blocking forms that assist in the whole fighting sequence. Doshin So introduced the locking of the joints, to immobilise the adversary for a predetermined period of time and grappling methods that could be used in unison with other applications. The grappling was probably a derivative of the Hakko-ryu, although the grappling methods can be witnessed in many Chinese martial art schools. Shorinji kempo contains numerous procedures that need to be learnt before one can be classed as a master grade, contained within a structured syllabus.

Body armour is worn in order that students can acquire ways of striking without the risk of severe injury. The protection is fundamental to the scholar having the opportunity to practise his skills and refine them accordingly. The fighting crafts are learnt often when the pupil is put in the sparring mode. The individual understands the importance of their stance and the posture in both attack and defence. Punches and kicks do not need to be controlled as much because of the body protection, which is seen as advantageous in the development of the disciple's power and speed.

Shorinji kempo has a worldwide membership and continually grows from strength to strength. Doshin So gave a good insight in how Chinese and Japanese forms can create an effective hybrid form that can be taught to students and masters alike.

SUIEI-JUTSU

Many Japanese martial arts needed to be of a specialist nature. One such specialised martial art was known as suiei-jutsu, or 'the art of swimming'. This martial art has interested historians and laymen alike for the astonishing skills that it contained. The form of survival whilst in the water and whilst submerged could have been a role requested of specialist fighting warriors. The warriors learnt how to cross a river and other water obstacles without being detected by the enemy on the other side of the crossing. Knowledge of several aspects needed to be observed.

Firstly, the pupil was educated in how to hold the air inside their lungs and how to accomplish this for much longer than the average swimmer. The warriors not only had to swim submerged, they also had to bear their weapons. They needed to come ashore fully prepared for battle and hold their positions until reinforcements came to their assistance. Therefore, the warrior not only had a need to be skilled at swimming but also be competent at fighting. An entire military operation could depend on the effective students of suiei-jutsu. The training and practice was rigorous and it was a specialised craft.

The soldier was also tutored on how to swim for long period of times in case they either faced a long crossing or they had to bide their time to emerge from the water at the best opportunity. They needed to be taught how to move silently and rapidly from the water. The element of surprise was of course crucial and an integral part of the operation.

A feudal lord would not only have archery ranges for his samurais to train in kyu-jutsu or fencing halls for ken-jutsu, but also several ponds to practise various swimming techniques. A riding samurai's mount also had to know how to swim and the discipline of oyogi-jutsu, the art of swimming in armour, was also learnt.

Suiei-jutsu has mostly died out due to the advancements in modern warfare. However, Japanese school programmes still contained specialist tests in the late nineteenth century and a military grading system of belts was used. It is believed that Jigaro Kano probably adopted this belt ranking system for judo, a method now employed by the vast majority of martial arts practised today. Those interested in traditional Japanese martial arts history should not overlook suei-jutsu as it formed an important role in a samurai's education.

SUMO

Sumo wrestling dates back nearly two thousand years and has been well written about. Sumo plays a significant part in the history of Japan, where the art has always been acclaimed and respected. The audiences fill to capacity on nearly every occasion that an event is due to take place.

Sumo wrestling has been well popularised by Japanese television and is eagerly watched by millions of people. The media has consequently created stars and a high status has been awarded to certain individuals. High-ranking and graded wrestlers have seen their standard of living increase in epic proportions, and they are well-respected celebrities in their home country. The mass media has helped in the general awareness of this martial art throughout the world and certain countries have their own competitions, but not on the scale of Japan. The expansion of sumo is slow, in terms of a global membership, as wrestlers are traditionally taken from an early age and almost devote all their early years to this subject.

Modern-day sumo wrestling is contested between opponents that can weigh in at over three hundred pounds. The wrestling takes place in an arena, known as a '*dohyo*'. The aim is to either force the opponent out of the area or to force him to touch the ground with any part of his anatomy above the knee. Pushing or throwing an opponent in a precise manner can achieve this goal.

Sumo wrestlers are additionally renowned for their incredible agility and for their phenomenal power and strength. The education of sumo comes from a fighter's stable, which is known as a *'beya'*. Here, the juniors are expected to serve those of a higher rank, as part of their apprenticeship. There is a hierarchy within the establishments and devotion is required for success.

Each wrestler wears a loincloth called a '*mawashi*' that is grabbed and held with a firm grip by the opponent. The *mawashi* serves to aid in the pushing and the throwing of the opponent as this acts as an anchor or pivot from where the moves are initiated.

The sumo wrestlers are known to consume a special and specifically created diet. The eating habits have been designed to increase stamina and the strength that the competitor can have. The food is specially prepared and contains all the vitamins and other nutritional ingredients that are considered and proven to have the desired result. Modern knowledge concerning nutrition is utilised to give the fighter that added edge when in the tournament scenario.

Tournaments, known as '*basho*', are regular throughout the calendar in Japan. This gives the opportunity for the wrestler to gain prize money and sponsorship deals. Special trophies are awarded to those that have achieved a high status.

TANTO-JUTSU

A *tanto* is a Japanese term for a dagger. This type of weapon featured in many military engagements and was employed by the *bushi* of the feudal periods throughout Japanese history. The *tanto* was an implement that served and gave the fighter another means of combat apart from the others that he may have selected to bear. The dagger enhances the overall fighting capabilities of the warrior whilst assisting in other chores that might be deemed appropriate for such a tool.

The Japanese warrior classes have been famed for their sword and weapon skills, whatever the chosen arm. They not only developed skills and crafts of how to use them on the battleground, but were also famous for the way they dedicated their study to them.

The Japanese have established many complete martial forms from a single item, a science that has been passed down through many generations. The Japanese hold many of their martial forms in high regard and are envied by many nations for their devotion and dedication to a single topic. The same can be said of tanto-jutsu and allied forms that have been around for many years.

The samurai that would use the dagger in conjunction with the sword frequently wore the *tanto*. The dagger was normally used should the sword have been lost in an engagement, and the art of fighting with it was a necessity. The dagger has many advantages and disadvantages when compared to other bladed weapons.

A dagger can be concealed and can be easily transported. It can be used at close-range and as well as being thrust, used in a roundhouse manner, used for downward and uppercut attacks and it can also be thrown if necessary. However, projecting the dagger was always viewed as the last and final resort, as a thrown weapon would mean the possibility of having no weapon at all and would demand a great deal of accuracy if the opponent was a long way off.

Tanto-jutsu is one of those many martial arts that have been absorbed into more popular forms. The student will often practise the skills with either the use of a rubber or wooden variety and only when mastery has been acquired will the student be permitted to train with the real item. The *tanto*, although not a popular weapon, is sometimes used in kata demonstrations and as part of other martial arts programmes, most notably Tomiki Aikido.

The targets are around the face, the neck and the throat regions, the chest, the stomach and numerous areas at the rear. In fact, the dagger will inflict potential damage no matter what area of the body that it hits.

YARI-JUTSU

Yari-jutsu translates as 'the art of the spear'. The spear has many uses that would have appealed to the warrior. Firstly, the weapon can be crafted to the requirements of the individual. The length and the weight can be made to individual design. The spear that was used on the battlefield was usually over ten feet in length. Secondly, a spear can be made cheaply and is therefore easily obtained.

The spear, or '*yari*', is made of a wooden shaft with a wooden or metal blade at one end. The blade would be crafted so that the base could be inserted into the shaft. The '*hoko*' was a spear where the blade would slot on the outside of the shaft.

The weapon can be handheld for hand-to-hand combat or thrown at an opponent. The shaft enabled close quarter combat to occur and the student is given an education in how to apply the strikes to one's counterpart in order to obtain the maximum results. Close quarter combat with a *yari* is a science that would be covered in depth and bear strong similarities to bo-jutsu and naginata-jutsu. The yari can be thrown at the opponent at long-range and was a particular favourite of the warrior classes when faced with an opponent on a horse. The generals would use the spear-wielding warriors in conjunction with the archers to reduce the levels of soldiers their swordsmen would have to face in hand-to-hand combat.

Yari-jutsu was to see a rapid decline in its membership with the introduction of firearms and allied explosive devices.

JAPANESE MARTIAL TERMS

JAPANESE MARTIAL TERMS

Please note your own particular school may use a different phrase or term from that supplied below. There are different terms used by different martial arts.

Age uke ~ rising block ~ when the block travels in an upward direction, usually to defend the top of the head from a downward attack

Age zuki ~ rising punch ~ a punch attack in an upward direction

Ai gamae ~ matching posture ~ opponents that have similar stance

Aite ~ training partner

Ai-uchi ~ simulutaneous score ~ a phrase used for simultaneous score in a competition; also a call made by a referee to indicate a simultaneous score in a competition

Antei ~ balance ~ this term denotes the manner in which the individual holds balance or should adopt it

Ashi barai ~ leg or foot sweep ~ a popular take down technique

Ashi sabaki ~ leg or foot movement

Ashi waza ~ leg or foot techniques

Ate ~ strike ~ refers to the manner and delivery of strike

Ato uke ~ feint and strike

Awase zuki ~ double punch ~ a double punch attack from various angles and positions

Bogu ~ armour ~ referring to some arts that wear full body armour

Bu ~ military

Budo ~ military way

Budokan ~ military way school ~ denotes any Japanese martial arts club

Bushi ~ warrior ~ term for the samurai

Bushido ~ warrior way ~ an unwritten code that was followed by the majority of the warrior classes and outlined the way the samurai would conduct their affairs in everyday life and during times of war. The bushido contains several elements, for example, honour and duty.

Chudan ~ middle body area ~ the area of the body from the neck to the hip

Chudan geri ~ middle body area kick

Chudan uke ~ middle body area block

Chudan zuki ~ middle body area punch

Dachi ~ stance ~ a general reference for the way one adopts a specific posture

Deshi ~ student

Do ~ way or path

Dogu ~ equipment

Fu antei ~ lack of balance

Fudo dachi ~ fixed stance

Gedan ~ lower body area ~ the body below the hip

Gedan barai ~ lower body area sweep ~ used by some schools to imply a lower block

Gedan kaki uke ~ lower hooking block

Gedan tsuki ~ lower body area thrust

Gedan uke ~ lower body area block

Geri ~ kick

Geri waza ~ kicking techniques

Geta ~ **clogs** ~ traditional Japanese attire

Gi ~ training suit

Gyaku ~ reverse

Gyaku mawashi geri ~ reverse roundhouse kick

Gyaku zuki ~ reverse punch

Hairakata ~ **entry methods** ~ the way to gain an advantage over the opponent

Haito uchi ~ inner or ridgehand strike

Hajime ~ begin

Hakama ~ **divided skirt** ~ traditional Japanese attire worn in some forms

Hanshi ~ high grade master

Hantei ~ judgement

Hara ~ abdomen

Harai ~ sweep

Hasumi zuki ~ scissors punch

Heisoku dachi ~ informal stance

Hidari ~ left

Hidari gamae ~ left posture

Hidari jigo-tai ~ left defensive posture

Hiraken ~ half-clenched fist

Hirate ~ fore-knuckle

Hiza geri ~ knee kick

Hombu ~ headquarters

Idori ~ seated defence

Ipponken ~ one-knuckle fist

Itami ~ pain

Jodan ~ high body area ~ the area above the neck

Jodan geri ~ high body area kick

Jodan uke ~ high body area block

Jodan zuki ~ high body area punch

Juji uke ~ cross-arm block

Kaeshi ~ to counter

Kakato geri ~ heel kick

Kake geri ~ hook kick

Kake uke ~ hook block

Kake zuki ~ hook punch

Kan ~ school

Katame ~ grappling

Katame waza ~ grappling techniques

Katsu ~ resuscitation

Keage ~ groin kick

Ki ~ spirit ~ a fundamental component of many schools of martial art. It is employed to increase power used against the opponent

Kiba dachi ~ horse or straddle stance

Kime ~ focus

Kin geri ~ groin kick

Kiru ~ to cut

Kohai ~ junior grade

Koken uke ~ bent wrist block

Kokutsu dachi ~ back-leaning stance

Kokyu ~ correct breathing methods

Kote waza ~ wrist techniques

Kumite ~ sparring

Kuzushi ~ balance breaking

Ma ai ~ distance

Mae ~ front

Mae ashi geri ~ front leg kick

Mae empi uchi ~ front elbow strike

Mae geri keage ~ front snap kick

Mae geri kekomi ~ front thrust kick

Mae tobi geri ~ front jump kick

Mae ukemi ~ front breakfall

Mairi ~ surrender

Makiwari ~ striking post ~ a karate training tool

Mawashi ~ roundhouse

Mawashi empi uchi ~ roundhouse elbow strike

Mawashi geri ~ roundhouse kick

Mawashi tobi geri ~ roundhouse jump kick

Mawashi zuki ~ roundhouse punch

Meijin ~ master

Migi ~ right

Migi gamae ~ right posture

Migi jigo-tai ~ right defensive posture

Mikazuki geri ~ crescent kick

Mu ~ clear mind

Nagashi zuki ~ flowing punch

Nami ashi ~ lower block kick

Nanami uchi ~ diagonal strike

Naotte ~ relax ~ a command to do so

Narande ~ line-up ~ a command to do so

Neko-ashi dachi ~ cat stance

Ne waza ~ ground fighting

Nihon ~ Japan

Nihon nukite ~ two-finger strike

Nukite ~ spear-hand

Obi ~ belt

Oi zuki ~ lunge punch

Osaekomi ~ holding ~ used to imply the correct way to hold the opponent once in a grappling position

Randori ~ free practice

Rei ~ to bow

Reigisaho ~ respect

Renzuki ~ continuous

Ritsurei ~ standing bow

Samurai ~ warrior class

Sanchin dachi ~ hour-glass stance

Seiken zuki ~ fore fist punch

Seiza ~ sit ~ usually a command to do so

Sempai ~ senior grade

Sensei ~ instructor

Shiai ~ contest

Shiatsu ~ back massage

Shime waza ~ choke or strangle techniques

Shimpan ~ referee

Shintai ~ motion

Shomen-ni-rei ~ bow to the front

Shotei uchi ~ palm-heel strike

Shotei uke ~ palm-heel block

Shuto uchi ~ outer or knife-hand strike

Shuto uke ~ outer or knife-hand block

Soto uke ~ outer block

Sune geri ~ shin kick

Tameshiwara ~ breaking

Tate empi uchi ~ vertical elbow strike

Tate shuto uchi ~ vertical open or knife-hand strike

Tate shuto uke ~ vertical open or knife-hand block

Tatte ~ to stand ~ usually a command to do so

Tegatana ~ hand-blade

Tenrankai ~ exhibition

Te-waza ~ hand techniques

Tobi geri ~ jump kick

Tori ~ defender

Tsuru ashi dachi ~ crane stance

Uchi ~ strike

Uchi uke ~ inner block

Uke ~ block

Uke ~ attacker

Ukemi ~ break fall

Undo ~ exercise

Ura ~ rear or back

Uraken uchi ~ back fist strike

Ushiro ashi geri ~ rear leg kick

Ushiro empi uchi ~ rear elbow strike

Ushiro geri ~ rear kick

Waza ~ techniques

Yame ~ stop

Yoi ~ ready

Yoko empi uchi ~ side elbow strike

Yoko geri ~ side kick

Yoko tobi geri ~ side jumping kick

Yoko ukemi ~ side breakfall

Yudansha ~ block belt holder

Zempo ukemi ~ front rolling break fall

Other titles from Summersdale

Goju-Ryu Karate-Do
KATA TENSHO
Ancient Form to Modern-Day Application

転掌

SHIHAN CHRIS ROWEN

BUNBUKAN
Institute of Classical Japanese Budo Culture

Kata Tensho
Ancient Form to Modern-Day Application
Shihan Chris Rowen
£12.99 Pb

Tensho, which literally means 'turning hands', is one of the two main forms of the Goju school of karate-do. This book covers 500 years of the history of this form together with 160 step-bystep illustrated instructions for its use today.

Shihan Chris Rowen, sixth dan, has a karate lineage which can be traced directly back to the fifteenth century. He has the honour and privilege of being one of the few westerners to be awarded a teaching certificate directly from the late legendary Grandmaster Yamaguchi Gogen, tenth dan in Goju-Ryu karate-do, having spent years studying at the Hombu Dojo in Japan. His studies led him to Okinawa where he studied Kobudo under the late master Akamine Etsuke and he is now in his fourth decade of martial arts training and teaching and third decade of practising Kata Tensho.

Shihan Rowen is the chief instructor of the Bunbukan Institute of Classical Japanese Budo Culture, which has branches around the world including England, Mauritius, France, Germany, Wales and America.

A highly regarded and sought-after instructor, the author is also a columnist whose work has featured in both the national and international press, and he has acted as a consultant on television, film and radio.

'*Chris Rowen's thorough and engaging study reveals Tensho to not only be beautiful and fascinating but also accessible and relevant*'

Jamie Clubb, Martial Arts Illustrated

'*Seeing Shihan Rowen perform Tensho, his mastery of the kata was revealed in every movement. Not only was I taken aback by his physical skills, his in-depth explanation of the kata and its applications were equally inspiring*'

Iain Abernethy, fifth dan

Foil Fencing

The techniques and tactics of modern foil fencing

Prof. John 'Jes' Smith

Foreword by
Keith A. Smith
President of the British Fencing Association

summersdale *sports*

Foil Fencing

The Techniques and Tactics of Modern Foil Fencing

Professor John 'Jes' Smith

£12.99 Pb

In this comprehensive guide to the practice and techniques of foil fencing, Professor John 'Jes' Smith, one of Britain's foremost fencing masters, provides an essential reference work to this fascinating sport. Informative and practical, *Foil Fencing* is illustrated with over 50 easy-to-follow diagrams, and offers expert advice on how to get the most out of your fencing training. Covering offensive and defensive strategies, established practices and more innovative modern concepts, *Foil Fencing* also includes sample demonstration exercises so that the reader, whether novice, experienced fencer or junior coach, can apply the material covered.

Professor John 'Jes' Smith is a Master of the British Academy of Fencing and a member of the Académie d'Armes International. He has taught at clubs, schools and colleges in London for many years.

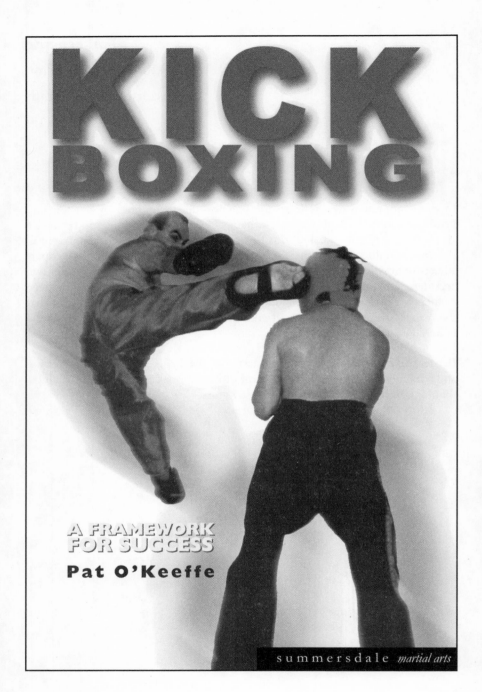

KICK BOXING

A FRAMEWORK FOR SUCCESS

Pat O'Keeffe

summersdale *martial arts*

Kick Boxing

A Framework for Success

Pat O'Keeffe

£12.99 Pb

Kick Boxing – A Framework for Success sets out, examines and defines the techniques, methods and practices that make up the training of a kick boxer.

Designed in a user-friendly and clear style, this is a fully comprehensive manual. It explains everything a novice needs to know to get started in the sport, and can also be used by experienced practitioners as a working reference to solve or re-examine problems of craft and skill.

The book covers the following topics:

- The fundamentals
- Secondary techniques
- Defence and counter-attack
- Combinations
- Timing, distance and mobility
- Sparring
- Speed and power
- Conditioning
- The schedule
- The coach
- The way beyond trophies
- Targets and techniques

Kick Boxing – A Framework for Success shows you how to achieve real results in simple steps.

Pat O' Keeffe is a successful trainer in kick boxing and is the British Head and Team Coach for the American Kick Boxing organisation, K.I.C.K. A renowned authority on the subject, he has fought numerous World Champions, including Rudi Van Damme and Nigel Benn.

KARATE'S
GRAPPLING METHODS

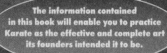

The information contained
in this book will enable you to practice
Karate as the effective and complete art
its founders intended it to be.

IAIN ABERNETHY

Karate's Grappling Methods

Understanding Kata & Bunkai

Iain Abernethy

£15.99 Pb

The book covers the following topics:

- Understanding kata and bunkai (applications)
- The role of grappling in self defence
- Close range strikes
- Throws and takedowns
- Ground fighting
- Chokes and strangles
- Arm bars
- Leg and ankle locks
- Neck wrenches
- Finger locks
- Wrist locks
- Fighting dirty
- Combinations
- Live grappling drills

Iain Abernethy has been involved in the martial arts since childhood. Iain holds a fifth dan in karate with the British Combat Association (one of the world's leading groups for close-quarter combat, self-protection and practical martial arts) and he is also a senior instructor for the British Karate-Do Chojinkai. Iain regularly writes for the UK's leading martial arts magazines and he is a member of the Combat Hall of Fame. One of the UK's leading exponents of applied karate, Iain has written a number of critically acclaimed books on the practical application of traditional martial arts and is well known for his work on the pragmatic use of the techniques and concepts recorded in the traditional kata. Iain's seminars, books, videos, DVDs and articles have proved to be very popular with those groups and individuals who wish to practise their arts as the pragmatic systems they were originally intended to be.

www.summersdale.com